PROGRAMMING FOR BEGINNERS 2025

Your Step-by-Step Journey to Coding
Proficiency with Engaging Projects and
Practical Exercises

GRANT D. HARPER

DISCLAIMER

This book is intended for educational and informational purposes only. While every effort has been made to ensure accuracy, the author and publisher do not guarantee that the information contained herein is free from errors or omissions. The author and publisher shall not be held liable for any damages, losses, or issues arising from the use or misuse of the content within this book. Readers are encouraged to verify any code, methods, or information provided and apply them responsibly. Use this book at your own discretion and proceed with caution when applying the concepts discussed.

DEDICATION

To all the aspiring programmers taking their first steps into the world of coding—this book is for you.

May your curiosity, perseverance, and creativity guide you through the challenges and joys of learning to program.

To my family and friends, whose unwavering support and encouragement continue to inspire me.

And to every teacher, mentor, and fellow learner who believes that knowledge should be accessible to all—thank you for making this journey possible.

HOW TO USE THIS BOOK

This book is designed to guide you from the very basics of programming to building real-world applications with clarity and confidence. Whether you are a complete beginner or someone looking to refresh your programming skills, this book provides a structured approach to help you master the fundamentals of programming.

What to Expect

The book is organized into clear, easy-to-follow chapters that gradually build your knowledge and skills. You will find:

- **Step-by-step explanations** of key concepts, ensuring you understand the foundational principles of programming.
- **Practical examples and exercises** to reinforce learning and help you apply what you've learned in real-world scenarios.
- **Projects and challenges** that encourage you to build your own programs, enhancing creativity and problem-solving abilities.

How to Approach This Book

- **Start from the Beginning:** If you are entirely new to programming, it is recommended to read the book from the start to build a solid foundation.
- **Skip Ahead if Necessary:** If you have some experience, feel free to jump to chapters that cover topics you are interested in or need to improve.

- **Practice as You Learn:** The hands-on exercises and projects are designed to be completed alongside your reading. The more you practice, the better you will retain the knowledge.
- **Refer Back as Needed:** This book is meant to be a resource you can return to whenever you need clarification or inspiration.

Tools You Will Need

- A computer with internet access.
- A code editor or Integrated Development Environment (IDE) suitable for your chosen programming language.
- Patience, curiosity, and a willingness to learn from mistakes.

Final Tip

Take your time, enjoy the learning process, and don't be afraid to experiment with the code. Programming is a skill that grows through practice, creativity, and persistence.

Now, let's dive in and start your journey to mastering programming.

TABLE OF CONTENTS

INTRODUCTION

Learning to program can feel overwhelming, especially if you're just starting out. With countless programming languages, syntax rules, and coding paradigms, it's easy to feel lost before you even write your first line of code. But here's the good news—programming doesn't have to be intimidating. With the right guidance and a structured approach, anyone can learn to code and start building practical, real-world applications.

This book is designed specifically for beginners who want to take their first steps into the world of programming. Whether you're aiming to start a career in tech, build your own apps, automate everyday tasks, or simply understand how software works, this book will provide you with the essential knowledge and skills to get started.

Why Learn Programming?

In today's digital world, programming has become an invaluable skill. It's not just for software developers—people in a wide range of professions can benefit from knowing how to code. Whether you want to automate repetitive tasks, analyze data, build websites, or create apps, programming empowers you to bring your ideas to life.

Learning to code also fosters problem-solving skills, logical thinking, and creativity. It trains your mind to break down complex problems into manageable parts, making it easier to develop solutions not just in code, but in everyday situations.

Who Is This Book For?

This book is designed for absolute beginners—no prior programming experience is needed. If you've ever felt intimidated by coding, struggled with technical jargon, or just didn't know where to start, this book will guide you step by step.

It's also suitable for individuals who may have dabbled in programming before but want a fresh start with a clear, structured approach. Whether you're a student, a professional looking to upskill, or simply someone curious about programming, you'll find practical and straightforward guidance here.

What Will You Learn?

This book covers the foundational concepts of programming in a clear, accessible way. You'll start with the very basics, such as understanding what programming is and how code works. As you progress, you'll learn about:

- **Programming Fundamentals:** Variables, data types, loops, conditionals, and functions.
- **Problem-Solving Techniques:** Breaking down problems and writing algorithms to solve them.
- **Real-World Applications:** Building small programs and projects to apply your knowledge practically.

- **Debugging and Optimization:** Finding and fixing errors, and making your code more efficient.
- **Best Practices:** Writing clean, readable, and maintainable code.

By the end of this book, you'll have a solid understanding of the core concepts and practical skills needed to start coding confidently. You'll be able to write basic programs, troubleshoot common errors, and understand how different programming concepts fit together.

A Hands-On Approach to Learning

This book takes a hands-on approach, combining theory with practice. Each chapter introduces key concepts, followed by examples and exercises that encourage you to apply what you've learned immediately. You'll also find practical projects that challenge your creativity and help you build real-world applications.

How to Make the Most of This Book

To gain the most from this book, practice consistently. Don't just read—code along, experiment with the examples, and try modifying the scripts to see what happens. The more you interact with the material, the deeper your understanding will become.

Programming is not just about memorizing syntax; it's about problem-solving, creativity, and perseverance. Mistakes are part of the learning process, and every error is an opportunity to grow. Embrace challenges, stay curious, and enjoy the journey of becoming a programmer.

Your Journey Begins Here

The world of programming is vast and constantly evolving, but every great programmer started as a beginner. This book is your starting point, and with dedication and practice, you'll be well on your way to mastering the fundamentals of coding.

Let's get started on your programming journey—one line of code at a time.

CHAPTER ONE

INTRODUCTION TO DATA ANALYSIS

The act of inspecting, cleaning, transforming, and modeling data with the intention to find relevant information and reaching a conclusion to boost the decision-making process is referred to as Data Analysis. There are different facets and techniques for data analysis. The data analysis in statistics is categorized into exploratory data analysis, confirmatory data analysis, and descriptive statistics. Data requires to be cleaned. Data cleaning is the procedure of fixing the outliers and other inaccurate and unwanted information. There are different types of data cleaning processes to use based on the type of data to be cleaned.

Business intelligence explores the data analysis that extends heavily on aggregation, slicing, disaggregation, dicing, and concentrating on the business information. Predictive analytics refers to the use of statistical models for predictive forecasting. Text analytics describes the application of statistical, structural models, and linguistic models to derive and categorize the information from texts. All these describe different varieties of data analysis.

Python for Data Analysis

Python is a simple, clear, and elaborate programming language. That is the reason many scientists and engineers go for Python to implement numerous applications. Probably they prefer handling the main task quickly rather than spend hundreds of hours mastering the nuances of a "complex" programming language.

This lets scientists, engineers, researchers, and analysts to dive into the project more quickly. As a result, they gain important insights into the minimum amount of time and resources. This does not imply that Python is fit and perfect programming language on where to complete data analysis and machine learning. Languages such as R may have advantages and properties Python doesn't have. However, Python is a good starting point, and you may attain the right knowledge of data analysis if you use it in future projects.

Comparism Between Python or R

You may have already come across this in Reddit, Stack Overflow, and other forums and websites. You may have also searched for other programming languages because even learning Python or R requires a few weeks and months. It is a huge time investment, and you don't want to make any mistake. To avoid any confusion, just begin with Python because the usual skills and concepts are easy to transfer to other languages. In some cases, you may need to adopt a whole new approach to thinking. But all in all, understanding how to apply Python in data analysis will provide you a channel to solve many complex problems.

Some may say that R is designed for statisticians, especially when it comes to easy and better data visualization properties. It's also easy to learn, especially if you plan to use it for data analysis. On the flipside, Python is a bit flexible because it goes past data analysis. Most data scientists and machine learning practitioners may have selected Python because the code they write can be integrated into a dynamic and live web application.

While it's open for debate, Python is still a great choice for beginners or anyone who wants to get started with data analysis and machine learning. It is quite easy to learn, and you can dive into full-time programming if you see that this suits you well.

Wide Spread Application of Data Analysis

There are a lot of packages and tools that enable the usage of Python in Data analysis and machine learning. Some of these packages consist of NumPy, scikit-learn, and Pandas. These tools simplify the data analysis process. Additionally, graduates from the university can dive into data science because most universities nowadays provide an introductory course in computer science with Python as the main programming language. The change from computer programming and software development can happen so fast because many people already have the correct foundation to begin learning and using programming to tackle real-world data problems.

Another reason for Python's popularity use is that there are numerous resources that will show you how to complete anything. If you've any questions, it is because someone else has requested that, and another solved it for you. This makes Python more popular because of the presence of resources online.

Clarity

Because of the ease of learning and Python's syntax clarity, experts can concentrate on the crucial features of their projects and problems. For instance, they can apply NumPy, TensorFlow, and scikit-learn to gain insights rather than build everything from scratch.

This generates another level of clarity because professionals can concentrate on the nature of the problem and its effects. They can also come up with effective approaches to handling the problem rather than being bombarded with the many challenges a given programming language presents. The main aim should always be on the challenge and the opportunities it may bring. It only requires a single breakthrough to change the entire thinking about a given problem, and Python can achieve that because of its ease and clarity.

The Types of Data Analysis

1. Descriptive Analysis

Data science is related to information retrieval and data collection approaches with the aim of reconstituting past events to determine patterns and identify insights that help determine what happened and what made it happen. For instance, looking at sales figures by region to identify customer preferences. This section requires that you remain familiar with statistics and data visualization approaches.

2. Predictive Analysis

Data science is a means to determine the chances that some events are currently taking place or will occur in the future. In the following case, the data scientist considers past data to determine explanatory variables and create statistical models that can be used in other data points. For instance, trying to predict the probability that a certain credit card transaction is fraudulent in real-time. This section is usually related to the machine learning field.

3. Prescriptive Analysis

In this case, data analysis is considered as a way to make informed decisions, or probably data- driven decisions. The focus should be to search for multiple options and applying simulation approaches and optimize the results. For instance, maximizing the supply chain by aiming to reduce the operating costs. Typically, descriptive data science aims to address the question of what does the data tell me. On the other hand, the predictive analysis answers the question of why is the data behaving in this way, and prescriptive analysis respond to the question of how you optimize the data toward a given goal.

CHAPTER TWO

INTRODUCTION TO PYTHON

In this chapter, we shall look at the Python programming language basic stuff. This chapter tries to teach you Python in brief. It's so much as a cheat sheet, so it will only remind you of some basic features to start you off. Typically, if you really want to master a language, you need to commit time and program it for a while. This chapter assumes that you're already familiar with Python programming and will, therefore, skip the majority of the non-language–specific stuff. The important keywords will be pointed out so you can easily spot them. We shall concentrate on Python 3 because that is the version you need to use. All the examples we shall provide to you are written in Python 3.

The Properties of Python Language

First, Python is a strongly typed language.

1. Getting help

Help in Python is usually available within the interpreter. If you want to learn how an object operates, all you need to do is call **help (<Object>)!** Additionally, the most important are dir. (), which displays all the object's methods, and **<object>. _doc_,** which displays all the documentation string. Let's set some expectations here, so you know where you're going. This is also to introduce the limitations of Python, data analysis, data science, and machine learning (and also the key differences). Let's start.

Data Analysis vs. Data Science vs. Machine Learning

Data Analysis and Data Science are almost the same because they share the same goal, which is to derive insights from data and use it for better decision-making. Often, data analysis is associated with using Microsoft Excel and other tools for summarizing data and finding patterns. On the other hand, data science is often associated with using programming to deal with massive data sets. In fact, data science became popular as a result of the generation of gigabytes of data coming from online sources and activities (search engines, social media). Being a data scientist sounds way cooler than being a data analyst. Although the job functions might be similar and overlapping, it all deals with discovering patterns and generating insights from data. It's also about asking intelligent questions about the nature of the data (e.g., Are data points form organic clusters? Is there really a connection between age and cancer?). What about machine learning? Often, the terms data science and machine learning are used interchangeably. That's because the latter is about "learning from data." When applying machine learning algorithms, the computer detects patterns and uses "what it learned" on new data. For instance, we want to know if a person will pay his debts. Luckily, we have a sizable dataset about different people who either paid his debt or not. We also have collected other data (creating customer profiles) such as age, income range, location, and occupation. When we apply the appropriate machine learning algorithm, the computer will learn from the data. We can then input new data (new info from a new applicant) and what the computer learned will be applied to that new data. We might then create a simple program that immediately evaluates whether a person will pay his debts or not based on his information (age, income range, location, and occupation). This is an example of using data to predict someone's likely behavior.

Possibilities

Learning from data opens a lot of possibilities, especially in predictions and optimizations. This has become a reality, thanks to the availability of massive datasets and superior computer processing power. We can now process data in gigabytes within a day using computers or cloud capabilities. Although data science and machine learning algorithms are still far from perfect, these are already useful in many applications such as image recognition, product recommendations, search engine rankings, and medical diagnosis. And to this moment, scientists and engineers around the globe continue to improve the accuracy and performance of their tools, models, and analysis.

The Drawbacks of Data Analysis and Machine Learning

You might have read from news and online articles that machine learning and advanced data analysis can change the fabric of society (automation, loss of jobs, universal basic income, artificial intelligence takeover). In fact, society is being changed right now. Behind the scenes, machine learning and continuous data analysis are at work especially in search engines, social media and e-commerce. Machine learning now makes it easier and faster to do the following:

- Are there human faces in the picture?
- Will a user click an ad? (Is it personalized and appealing to him/her?)
- How to create accurate captions on YouTube videos? (recognize speech and translate into text)
- Will an engine or component fail? (preventive maintenance in manufacturing) • Is a transaction fraudulent?
- Is an email spam or not?

These are made possible by the availability of massive datasets and great processing power. However, advanced data analysis using Python (and machine learning) is not magic. It's not the solution to all problems. That's because the accuracy and performance of our tools and models heavily depend on the integrity of data and our own skill and judgment. Yes, computers and algorithms are great at providing answers. But it's also about asking the right questions. Those intelligent questions will come from us humans. It also depends on us if we'll use the answers being provided by our computers.

Accuracy & Performance

The most common use of data analysis is in successful predictions (forecasting) and optimization. Will the demand for our product increase in the next five years? What are the optimal routes for deliveries that lead to the lowest operational costs? That's why an accuracy improvement of even just 1% can translate into millions of dollars of additional revenues. For instance, big stores can stock up certain products in advance if the results of the analysis predict an increasing demand. Shipping and logistics can also better plan the routes and schedules for lower fuel usage and faster deliveries. Aside from improving accuracy, another priority is on ensuring reliable performance. How can our analysis perform on new data sets? Should we consider other factors when analyzing the data and making predictions? Our work should always produce consistently accurate results. Otherwise, it's not scientific at all because the results are not reproducible. We might as well shoot in the dark instead of making ourselves exhausted in sophisticated data analysis. Apart from successful forecasting and optimization, proper data analysis can also help us uncover opportunities. Later, we can realize that what we did is also applicable to other projects and fields. We can also detect outliers and interesting patterns if we dig deep enough. For example, perhaps, customers congregate in clusters that are big enough for us to explore and tap into. Maybe there are unusually higher concentrations of customers that fall into a certain income range or spending level. Those are just typical examples of the applications of proper data analysis. In the next chapter, let's discuss one of the most used examples in illustrating the promising potential of data analysis and machine learning. We'll also discuss its implications and the opportunities it presents.

CHAPTER THREE

IMPORTANT PYTHON LIBARIES

You can get a mind map describing software that can be used to analyze data at xmind.net. However, you cannot install all of this software in this chapter. This chapter will explore how to install SciPy, matplotlib, NumPy, and IPython on different platforms. You will also see some sample code that used NumPy.

- **NumPy** is a powerful Python library that features numerical arrays and functions.

- **SciPy** is a powerful Python library, which slightly overlaps NumPy. NumPy and SciPy historically shared their code but were later separated.

- **Matplotlib** provides a plotting library featuring NumPy. You will learn more about matplotlib during data visualization.

- **IPython** contains an architecture for interactive computing. The most critical part of the following project is the IPython shell. You will learn more about the IPython shell in the following chapter.

The installation instructions for the rest of the software will be provided in the rest of the book. When you're done reading this chapter, you will identify pointers on how to determine extra information online if you stumble or are uncertain about the right way to solve problems. This book uses applications based on Python, so that is why you need to have Python installed on your computer. Some operating systems come with Python already installed, but you will need to check whether the Python version is compatible with the software version you want to install. There are different Python implementations. In the following book, we shall stick to the standard CPython implementation, which is considered compatible with NumPy. The software application that we will install in this chapter features binary installers for Windows, Mac OS X, and Linux distributions. There are still source distributions in case you prefer that.

Installing the Software and Setting Up

You will learn how to install and set up NumPy, matplotlib, and IPython on Linux, Windows, and Mac OS X. Let's explore the process in detail.

For Windows

When you want to install the above Python libraries on a Windows operating system, it's a straightforward process that we dive into detail. You only require to download an installer, and a wizard will direct you through the installation steps. We will provide you with the steps to install NumPy. The steps to install the remaining libraries are the same. The instructions to use are as follows:

- Get a Windows installer from the Source Forge website or any other legit website. The current versions may change, so just select the one that suits your setup best.

- Select the right version from the available list.

- Next, open the EXE installer by double-clicking it.

- Next, you will see a description of NumPy and its properties. Now, click on the Next button.

NumPy Arrays

Once you are through with the installation of NumPy, now is the time to explore NumPy arrays. NumPy arrays are more efficient compared to Python lists when it comes to numerical operations. NumPy arrays are specialized objects that have broad optimization. NumPy code demands less explicit loops than equivalent Python code.

If we recall some of the mathematics topics you did learn in high school, I am sure you can remember scalars and vectors. For example, the number 2 is a scalar. When you add 3 to 2, you will be doing a scalar addition. We can create a vector out of a group of scalars. In Python programming, you will have a one-dimensional array. This concept can still be extended to a higher dimension. Conducting an operation on two arrays, like addition, can be reduced to a group of scalar computations.

In summary, NumPy is faster than the pure Python code. One thing that is clear, you can acquire the same results whether you use NumPy or not. But the result displayed differs in presentation. Remember that the result from the NumPysum () function doesn't have a lot of commas. This is because you are not working with a Python list but with a NumPy array.

Using IPython as a Shell

Data analysts, engineers, and scientists like to experiment. IPython was built by scientists with the goal of experimentation. The interactive environment provided by IPython is considered by many as a direct solution to MATLAB.

Below is a list of properties of the IPython shell:

- History mechanism
- The pylab switch
- Tab completion, which helps you identify a command
- Access to Python debugger and profiler

Web Scraping Using Python Libraries

In this section, you will scrape the "Rate My Professor" website. A brief description of Rate My Professor website, it's a website that has ratings of schools, professors, and universities. In this website, you can search for any professor or school and see their ratings before registering their courses. It is a great feature that helps you to learn more about your professor or the university that you wish to join. In this section, you will learn how to scrape and extract crucial professor's tag. While this is not an illegal process, mass scraping of data from this website may result in your

IP address being blacklisted. So, you should only attempt it once or twice, but don't do it foolishly.

Web Scraping

Also known as scraping, data harvesting, or data extraction is a mechanism used to mine data from websites. In some cases, web scraping can be vital when you get the data that you are searching for straight from the web, but sometimes, it is a bad way to handle it because it's like stealing the expensive data from the website without their permission. However, you should reduce your scraping process to only once or twice so that you don't fall in trouble.

The most important libraries for web scraping include:

1. Beautiful soup
2. Requests

Here are the steps that we would be following.

1. First, we import the relevant libraries
2. Finding the URL and keeping it in a variable
3. Sending a request to the website using the requests library
4. Applying the Beautiful Soup library to find the HTML data from the website.
5. Using soup to identify all methods to get the necessary tag that we are searching for.
6. Removing all the HTML tags and converting it to a plain text format.

You may be wondering the type of tags to extract, well in the Rate My Professor website, every professor has his or her respected tags. We will try to extract these tags. Before we start, ensure that you scrape the data at a low pace, and you can use a VPN service to change your IP address. This prevents your IP address from being blocked. Hope you will follow the instructions. One thing that you should note is that there is no need to explain each and every line of code because Python code is self-explanatory. But you will not be confused because everything will be made clear in an easy format. So, this guide is written in such a way that everybody can understand regardless of their programming level.

You may find a lot of online tutorials, but this guide is easy to understand because the codes are explained. However, some parts are a mechanical process, wherein you need to follow them.

Let's dive in!

First, import the necessary libraries

1. Let us import several libraries such as Beautiful Soup and Requests.

import requests

from bs4 import Beautiful Soup

2. Find the URL and store it in a variable

Let store the professor's URL within a variable called "url".

3. Send a request to the website using the requests library

In the following case, we apply the requests library by passing "url" as the parameter. Be careful that you don't run this numerous times. If you receive like Response 200, then it's a success. If you find something different, then there is something wrong with maybe the code or your browser.

4. Apply the Beautiful Soup library to get the raw HTML data from the website.

Here, we apply the Beautiful Soup by passing the page text as a parameter and applying the HTML parser. You can attempt to output the soup, but displaying the soup doesn't provide you the response. Instead, it contains a huge percentage of HTML data.

Here is a code snippet.

Therefore, you get the above information that you are looking for. You get all the tags of the professor. This is how you scrape the data from the internet using Requests and Beautiful Soup libraries. In summary, Python has three core data science libraries which many others have been built:

For simplicity, you can consider NumPy as your one-stop for arrays. NumPy arrays are different from the typical Python lists in many different ways, but a few to recall is that they are faster, consume less space, and have more functionality. It is important to remember, though, that these arrays are of a fixed size and type, which you define at creation. No infinitely appending new values like you want with a list.

CHAPTER FOUR

DATA MANIPULATION

The Python Pandas library is an open-source project that has easy to use tools for data manipulation and analysis. A significant amount of time in any machine learning project will be required to prepare the data and analyze the basic trends and patterns before creating any models. The Pandas library has risen into a powerhouse of data manipulation tasks in Python because it was built in 2008. With its elaborate syntax and flexible data structure, it's easy to learn and support faster data computation. The development of NumPy and Pandas library has stretched Python's multi-purpose nature to compute machine learning challenges. The acceptance of Python language in machine learning has been critical since then. This is one of the reasons highlighting the need for you to master these libraries. In the following chapter, you will learn about how to use NumPy and Pandas libraries for data manipulation from scratch. We shall mix both theory and practical aspects. First, we will recap the syntax and commonly used functions of the respective libraries. Then later work on a real-life data set. So, you need to be good at the basics of Python. No further knowledge is required. Also, ensure you have Python installed in your machine.

Key Things You Need to Know About NumPy and Pandas

- The data properties of Pandas are designed on top of the NumPy library. In one way, NumPy is a dependency of the Pandas library.

- Pandas is perfect at handling tabular data sets made of unique variables. Besides that, the Pandas library can still be used to perform even the most naïve of tasks such as loading data or performing feature engineering on time series data.

- NumPy is suitable for performing basic numerical computations like median, range, mean, etc. Besides that, it supports the development of multidimensional arrays.

- The NumPy library can also be used to mix C/C++ and Fortran code.

- Keep in mind, Python is a zero-indexing language, unlike R language, where indexing begins at one.

- The best thing about learning Pandas and NumPy is the strong, active community support you gain from the world.

Just to give you a grasp of the NumPy library, we'll quickly revise its syntax structures and some critical commands such as indexing, slicing, concatenation, etc. All these commands will be useful when using Pandas. Let's get started.

Getting Started with NumPy

First, load the library and confirm its version, just to be sure that we are not using an older version.

```
import NumPy as np

np.__version__

'1.12.1'
```

Next, build a list of numbers running from 0 to 9.

```
L = list(range(10))
```

Then convert integers to a string. This method of working with lists is known as a list comprehension.

List comprehension provides a versatile means to deal with list manipulation tasks easily.

Array Indexing

The important thing to remember is that indexing in Python starts at zero.

```
x1 = np.array([4, 3, 4, 4, 8, 4])

x1

array([4, 3, 4, 4, 8, 4])
```

#assess value to index zero

x1[0]

4

#assess fifth value

x1[4]

8

#get the last value

x1[-1]

4

#get the second last value

x1[-2]

8

#in a multidimensional array, we need to specify row and column index

x2

array([[3, 7, 5, 5],

[0, 1, 5, 9],

[3, 0, 5, 0]])

#1st row and 2nd column value

x2[2,3]

0

#3rd row and last value from the 3rd column

x2[2,-1]

0

#replace value at 0,0 index

x2[0,0] = 12

x2

array([[12, 7, 5, 5],

[0, 1, 5, 9],

[3, 0, 5, 0]])

Array Slicing

Now, we'll learn to access multiple or a range of elements from an array.

```
y = np.arange(10)

y

array([0, 1, 2, 3, 4, 5, 6, 7, 8, 9])
```

```
#from start to 4th position

y[:5]

array([0, 1, 2, 3, 4])
```

```
#from 4th position to end

y[4:]

array([4, 5, 6, 7, 8, 9])
```

```
#from 4th to 6th position

y[4:7]

array([4, 5, 6])
```

```
#return elements at even place

y[ : : 2]

array([0, 2, 4, 6, 8])
```

#return elements from first position step by two

y[1::2]

array([1, 3, 5, 7, 9])

#reverse the array

y[::-1]

array([9, 8, 7, 6, 5, 4, 3, 2, 1, 0]

Array Concatenation

Many a time, we are required to combine different arrays. So, instead of typing each of their elements manually, you can use array concatenation to handle such tasks easily.

#Using its axis parameter, you can define row-wise or column-wise matrix

np.concatenate([grid,grid],axis=1)

array([[1, 2, 3, 1, 2, 3],

[4, 5, 6, 4, 5, 6]])

Until now, we used the concatenation function of arrays of equal dimension. But, what if you are required to combine a 2D array with a 1D array? In such situations, np.concatenate might not be the best option to use. Instead, you can use np.vstack or np.hstack to do the task. Let's see how!

x = np.array([3,4,5])

grid = np.array([[1,2,3],[17,18,19]])

np.vstack([x,grid])

array([[3, 4, 5],

[1, 2, 3],

[17, 18, 19]])

#Similarly, you can add an array using np.hstack

z = np.array([[9],[9]])

np.hstack([grid,z])

array([[1, 2, 3, 9],

[17, 18, 19, 9]])

Besides the functions we have learned above, there are other mathematical functions available in the NumPy library, such as divide, multiple, mod, sin, cos, var, min, max, abs, etc. which you can apply to complete basic arithmetic calculations. Be free to go back to NumPy documentation for additional information on such functions. Let's proceed to Pandas now. Ensure you follow every line below because it will enable you to perform the computation using Pandas.

Getting Started with Pandas

The load library - pd is just an alias. The pd is used because it's short and literally abbreviates Pandas. Still, you can use any name as an alias.

import Pandas as pd

Next, create a data frame. Dictionary is used here where keys get converted to column names and values to row values.

data = pd.Data Frame ({'Country': ['Russia','Colombia','Chile','Equador','Nigeria'], 'Rank':[121,40,100,130,11]})

data

	Country	Rank
0	Russia	121
1	Columbia	40

2	Chile	100
3	Equador	130
4	Nigeria	11

We can perform a quick analysis of any data set using:

data.describe()

	Rank
count	5.000000
mean	80.400000
Std	52.300096
Min	11.00000
25%	40.000000
50%	100.000000
75%	121.000000
max	130.000000

Remember, describe () method performs summary statistics of integer/double variables. To find complete information about the data set, we can apply the info () function.

Among other things, it shows the data set has 5 rows and 2 columns with their respective names.

#Let's create another data frame.

data = pd.Data Frame ({'group':['a', 'a', 'a', 'b','b', 'b', 'c', 'c','c'],'ounces':[4, 3, 12, 6, 7.5, 8, 3, 5, 6]})

data

#Let's sort the data frame by ounces - inplace = True will make changes to the data
data.sort_values(by=['ounces'],ascending=True,inplace=False)

	group	ounces
1	a	3.0
6	c	3.0
0	a	4.0
7	c	5.0
3	b	6.0
8	c	6.0
4	b	7.5

| 5 | b | 8.0 |
| 2 | a | 12.0 |

Still, you can sort the data by not just one column but numerous columns as well.

data.sort_values(by=['group','ounces'],ascending=[True,False],inplace=False)

	group	Ounces
2	a	12.0
0	a	4.0
1	a	3.0
5	b	8.0
4	b	7.5
3	b	6.0
8	c	6.0
7	c	5.0
6	c	3.0

Typically, we get data sets with duplicate rows, which are just noise. As a result, before we train the model, we need to ensure we eliminate such inconsistencies within the data set. Here is how we can remove duplicate rows.

#sort values data.sort_values(by='k2')

	K1	K2
2	one	3
1	one	2
0	one	1
3	two	3
4	two	3
5	two	4
6	two	4

#remove duplicates - ta da! data.drop_duplicates()

Here, we removed duplicates based on matching row values across all columns. Alternatively, we can also remove duplicates based on a particular column. Let's remove duplicate values from the k1 column.

data.drop_duplicates(subset='k1')

	K1	K2
o	one	3
3	two	3

Now, we will learn to categorize rows based on a predefined criterion. It happens a lot while data processing where you need to categorize a variable. For example, say we have got a column with country names, and we want to create a new variable 'continent' based on these country names.

In this case, we will follow these steps:

```python
data = pd.DataFrame({'food': ['bacon', 'pulled pork', 'bacon',
 'Pastrami','corned beef', 'Bacon', 'pastrami', 'honey ham','nova lox'],
                'ounces': [4, 3, 12, 6, 7.5, 8, 3, 5, 6]})
data
```

Now, we want to create a new variable that indicates the type of animal which acts as the source of the food. To do that, first, we'll create a dictionary to map the food to the animals. Then, we'll use map function to map the dictionary's values to the keys. Let's see how is it done.

```
meat_to_animal = {
'bacon': 'pig',
'pulled pork': 'pig',
'pastrami': 'cow',
'corned beef': 'cow',
'honey ham': 'pig',
'nova lox': 'salmon'
}
```

```
def meat_2_animal(series):

if series['food'] == 'bacon':

return 'pig'

elif series['food'] == 'pulled pork':

return 'pig'

elif series['food'] == 'pastrami':

return 'cow'

elif series['food'] == 'corned beef':

return 'cow'

elif series['food'] == 'honey ham':

return 'pig' else:

return 'salmon'
```

Another method to create a new variable is by using the assign function. With the following tutorial, you can continue to discover the new functions, and you will learn how powerful Pandas are.

data.assign(new_variable = data ['ounces']*10

We constantly find missing values within the data set. A quick approach for inputting missing values is by completing the missing value using any random number. Not only missing values, but you may find a lot of outliers within your data set, which demands replacement.

Let's proceed and learn about grouping data and creating pivots in Pandas. It's an immensely important data analysis method which you'd probably have to use on every data set you work with.

Importing Data

Pandas has tools to help read data from an extensive source. Since the dataset being used is a csv file, you will require to access read_csv function. This function has numerous options for parsing data. In a lot of files, the default choice works well.

```
import pandas as pd
train_values = pd.read_csv('train_values.csv')
train_labels = pd.read_csv('train_labels.csv')
```

For data to be analyzed, it is important to train the values and labels into a single data frame. Pandas deliver a merge function that will integrate data frames on either indexes or columns.

Missing Data

Pandas has multiple functions to handle missing data. To begin with, the isna() function can be important to learn the number of missing values present in the data. The basic function of this appears at each value within a row and column, and it will display True if it is absent and false in case it is not. Therefore, it is possible to create a function that displays the fraction of missing values in every column.

In our dataset, there are no missing values available. But in case it was present, then we could apply a function to replace another value, or a function to remove the rows featuring missing values. Anytime you apply fillna(), you have several options. You can decide to replace it with a static value which can be a string or a number. Also, you can substitute it with computations. It is true that you will need to apply different techniques for various columns based on the types of data and missing values.

The following code illustrates how you can apply pandas functions to fill the numerical values using mean.

```
train[train.select_dtypes(include=['int64', 'float64']).columns] =
train[train.select_dtypes(include=['int64', 'float64']).columns].apply(lambda x:x.fillna(x.mean()))
```

Visualize the Data

When you plot values in Pandas, it doesn't appear attractive. However, if you want to highlight trends from data, it can always be the most effective means to achieve this. The basic function for plotting that is normally used is the plt.plot(). Whenever you plot in Pandas, you will need to refer to the matplotlib API. Therefore, it is critical that you use matplotlib first.

This function supports different visualization types, including histograms, boxplots, and scatter plots. Where the plotting function in Pandas becomes critical is when you use it with other data aggregation functions. To integrate the value_counts() using bar plot choice provides a rapid visualization for specific features. In the following code, we are exploring the distribution using this method.

```
import matplotlib.pyplot as plt
% matplotlib inlinetrain['thal'].value_counts().plot.bar()
```

When you apply the groupby function, you require to plot mean.

```
train.groupby("slope_of_peak_exercise_st_segment")['resting_blood_pressure'].mean().plot(kind='bar')
```

The Pandas pivot tables can still be used to create visualizations of compiled data. In this example, a comparison is made, and the relationship to heart disease available.

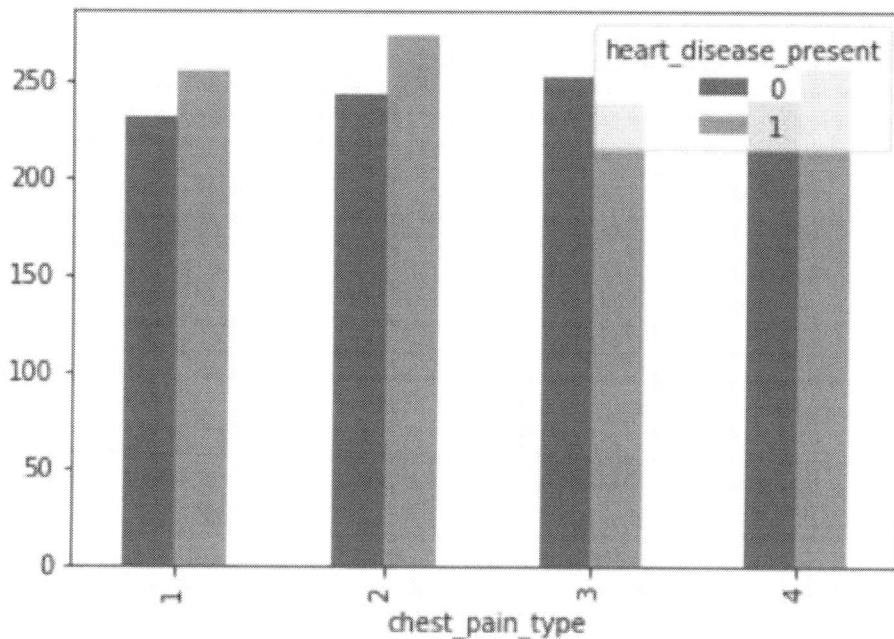

Transformation of Feature

Pandas does have different functions that can be applied in feature transformations. For instance, the most popular machine learning libraries expect data to be in numerical form. As a result, it is important to change any non-numeric properties. The right way to achieve this is by hot encoding. Pandas have a function for this known as the get dummies. Once this method is applied to a data column, it changes every unique value into a new binary column.

Another style which a feature may require to be converted for machine learning is called binning. A great example of this data set is the age feature. It can be significant to gather the ages into ranges for the model to learn. Pandas do have a function pd.cut that can be applied.

```
bins = [0, 30, 40, 50, 60, 70, 100]
train['age_group'] = pd.cut(train['age'], bins)
train['age_group'].value_counts().plot(kind='bar')
```

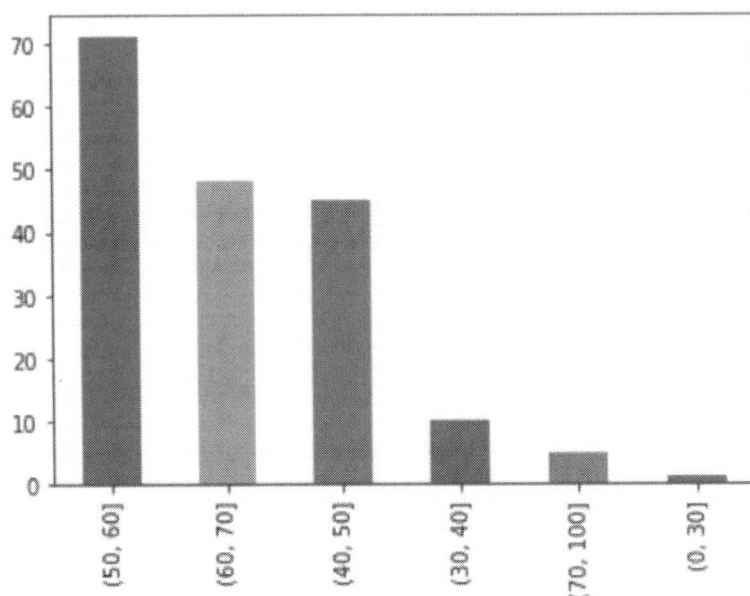

This is only a small introduction to different properties in Pandas for application in the early parts of the machine learning project. There are a lot of features to data analysis, manipulation, and the Pandas library itself. This can be a time-consuming stage, and Pandas deliver different tools and functions that can make the process efficient.

CHAPTER FIVE

DATA AGGREGATION

This represents the first part of aggregation and clustering using Pharo Data Frame. This will only handle the basic functionality like clustering a data series using values of a separate series of corresponding size and using aggregation functions to the grouped data structures.

The next iterations will deal with functionality extended based on the targeted scenarios. The implementation is likely to change into something optimized.

Definition of Data Frame

This represents spreadsheet such as data structures that deliver an API for cleaning, slicing, and analyzing data. In case you want to read more about the Data Frame project, you need to consider the documentation.

Split-Apply-Combine

The split-apply-combine is a technique where you categorize a certain task into manageable parts and then integrate all the parts together. The data aggregation and grouping facilitate the production of summaries for analysis and display. For example, when you calculate the average values or creating a table of counts. This is a step that adheres the split-apply-combine procedure.

1. Separate the data into sections based on a given procedure.
2. Use the function to every cluster independently.
3. Combine the results using a data structure.

Implementation

In this part, you will discover how the grouping and aggregation function is being implemented. In case you don't want these details, you can skip to the next part. Take, for instance, this message that has been sent to firstSeries object:

```
firstSeries groupBy: secondSeries.
```

Once this message is sent, first Series will define an object of Data Series Grouped, which divides first Series into various subseries depending on the values of second Series. The collection of subseries is later kept as an object of Data Series whose keys are equivalent to the special values of the second Series and values store the subseries of first Series. That will match each of those unique values.

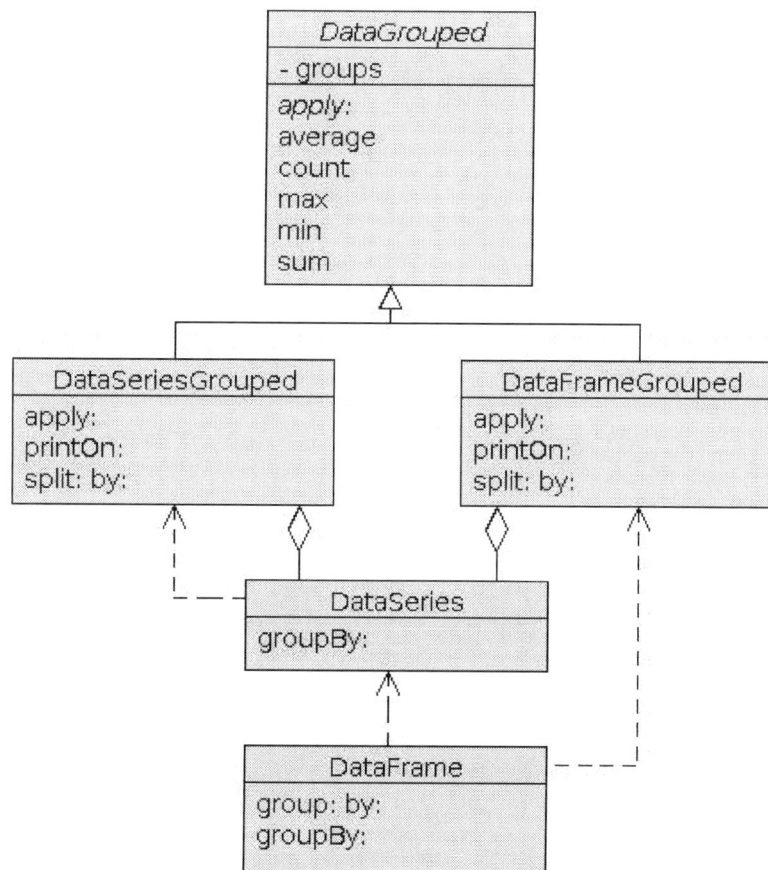

When a receiver of a group by: message is a Data Frame, it creates an instance of Data Frame Grouped, which splits the data similarly to the way Data Series Group does it, except the values of groups series are sub-data frames, not subseries.

This means groups represent Data Series that hold keys that match the unique values contained in a series which the data frame is identified. Where the data frame is categorized by a single column, this column is removed from data frame before the grouping. Therefore, this eliminates data duplication because the same values will be kept as keys.

For the case of Data Series Grouped, every subseries will be attached to a scalar, and all the following scalars will be joined into a Data Series. When it comes to the Data Frame Grouped, it will include the block to every column of each sub-data frame and display the eventual matrix of scalars as a new Data Frame. Aggregation happens with the use of messages. It requires a block as an argument, and uses it on every value of the group's series, and then integrates into a new data structure.

The most common aggregation functions, such as average, min, and max deliver shorter messages. In the following iteration, these messages are useful and work as shortcuts.

```
average
    ^ self apply: [ :each | each average ].
```

However, these messages will carry the optimized implementations of the likened aggregations because it is necessary that these functions are time and memory efficient. Let's examine the grouping series.

The easiest example of using this group by operator is to classify the values of a series using values of the same size.

```
bill := tips column: #total_bill.
sex := tips column: #sex.bill groupBy: sex.
```

The result of the above query will be an object. This object will separate the bill into two series. Because a lot of time, you need to classify the group series that resemble columns of a single data frame. There is a useful shortcut.

How to Group Data Frames?

Besides the shortcut for classifying columns. The Data Frame has a method for classifying one of its columns. The response of the above query will be an object of Data Frame Grouped, keeping two different data frames for smokers and non-smokers. The smoker column will be removed from the above data frames because its values will be kept as keys within a Data Frame Grouped object. Additionally, the different groups of smokers and non-smokers will enable the complete reconstruction of the smoker column when needed.

The aggregation functions represent the ones that accept different input and display a scalar value that sums up the values of that particular series. These refer to statistical functions such as min, max, stdev, and many more. Once the data has been combined, next you can use aggregation function to get the integrated data structure that sums up the original data.

```
grouped := tips group: #total_bill by: #day.
grouped apply: [ :each | each average round: 2].
```

Since the grouping is being done to a column of Data Frame by a separate column, the result will be a Data Series object. As said before, the Data Grouped presents shortcuts for popularly applied aggregation functions such as count, sum, min, and max. At the moment, these are shortcuts, but in future, they will execute the optimized aggregations that will be used faster.

Once the data frame was grouped into an object of Data Frame Grouped, we can also apply an aggregation function to this object. Data Frame Grouped implements the apply: message in such a way that the function is applied to each column of each sub-data frame, producing the scalar value. These scalars are then combined into a new data frame. The result of this query will be a data frame containing the number of non-empty cells for each column, corresponding to 'Male' and 'Female' rows

	total_bill	tip	smoker	day	time	size
Female	87	87	87	87	87	87
Male	157	157	157	157	157	157

CHAPTER SIX

HOW TO USE SCIKIT LEARN

Now that you are done with the installations, you can begin to use the libraries. We will begin with the Scikit-Learn library. To be able to use scikit-learn in your code, you should first import it by running this statement: **import sklearn**

Loading Datasets

Machine learning is all about analyzing sets of data. Before this, we should first load the dataset into our workspace. The library comes loaded with a number of datasets that we can load and work with. We will demonstrate this by using a dataset known as *Iris*. This is a dataset of flowers. The following code shows how we can use scikit-learn to load the dataset:

```python
# Import scikit-learn library
from sklearn import datasets
# Load iris dataset
iris= datasets.load_iris()
# Confirm by printing the shape of the data
print(iris.data.shape)
```

Simple Linear Regression

We need to use our previous example, which is, predicting the number of marks a student will score in a test depending on the number of hours they have studied for the test. It is a simple linear regression task since we only have two variables.

Import Libraries

Run the following Python statements tom import all the necessary libraries:

```python
import numpy as np
import pandas as pd

import matplotlib.pyplot as plt
```

This file is saved in an MS Excel file named *student_marks.csv*. It's in the directory where my Python scripts are found, so no need to give the path leading to the file. The .csv extension in the filename shows that it is a comma-separated values file.

The following statement will help us to import the dataset into the workspace. We are using the Pandas library (we imported it as *pd*) for this:

```python
dataset = pd.read_csv('student_marks.csv')
```

We can now explore the dataset to know more about it and see what it has. Go directly to the Python terminal and type this:

dataset.shape

Which means that the dataset has 25 rows and 2 columns. To see the first five rows of the data, call *head()* function.

However, you may get an error when you attempt to print the data. The cause of the error could be that Pandas is looking for the amount of information to display, so you should provide *sys* output information. The error can be solved by modifying your code to the following:

```python
import numpy as np
import pandas as pd
import matplotlib.pyplot as plt
import sys
sys.__stdout__ = sys.stdout
dataset = pd.read_csv('student_marks.csv')
print(dataset.head())
```

We have simply provided the information to the *sys* library. To see the statistical details of the dataset, we call the *describe()* function as follows:

dataset.describe()

We can now plot the data points on a 2-D graph and see how they are distributed. You no appreciate why we imported the *Matplotlib* library. The following code will help you to plot the

data points:

```
dataset.plot(x='Hours', y='Marks', style='o')
plt.title('Hours vs Marks(%)')
plt.xlabel('Hours')
plt.ylabel('Marks (%)')
plt.show()
```

The code returns the following plot:

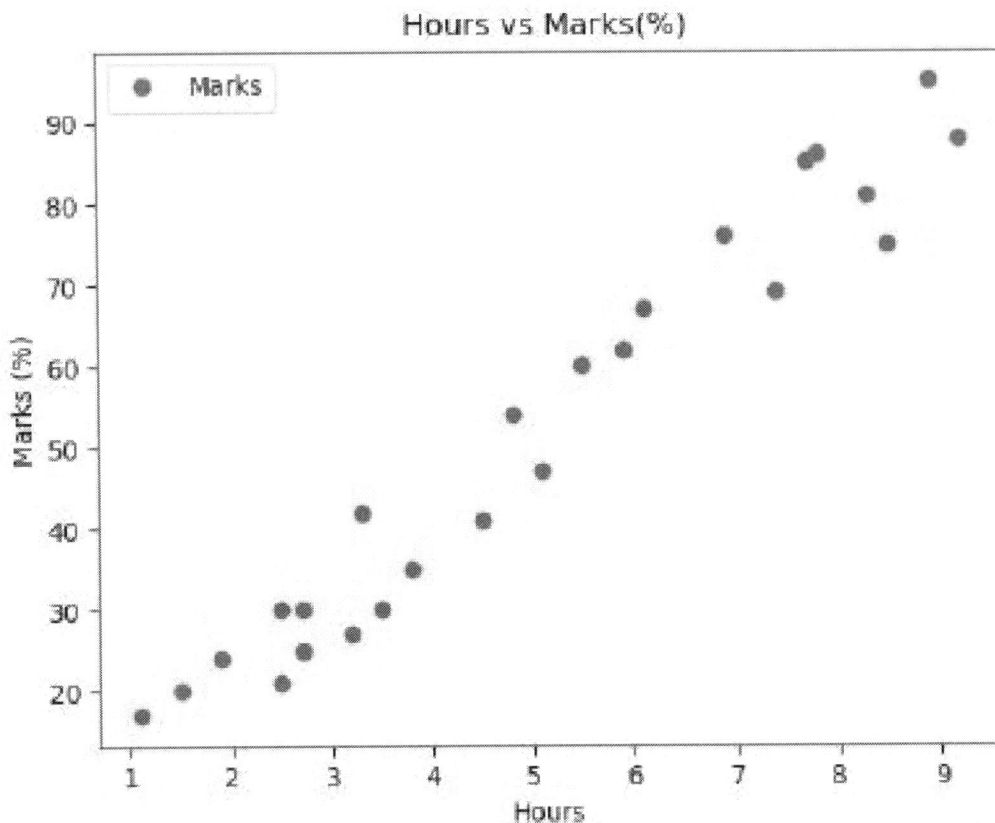

We have called the *plot()* function provided by the Pandas library. We passed the column names to this function, and it was able to create and display the plot. The *show()* function helped us to display the plot.

Data Preparation

The preparation of the data should involve subdividing it into labels and *attributes*. Attributes should create independent variables, and labels create dependent variables. Our dataset has only two columns. We are predicting Marks based on Hours. This means Hours will form the attribute while Marks will form the label. The attributes and labels can be extracted by running the following code:

```
X = dataset.iloc[:, :-1].values
y = dataset.iloc[:, 1].values
```

The X variable will store the attributes. Note that we have used -1 because we need all columns to be assigned to attributes except the last one, that is, Marks. The y variable will store the labels. Here, we have used 1 since the column for Marks is at index 1. Remember that column indexes begin at index 0. At this point, we have the attributes and labels for the dataset. We need to divide our data into two sets, namely the *training* and *test* sets. The Scikit- Learn library provides us with a method named "train_test_split()" which can be used for this.

Training the Algorithm

We will be training the algorithm using the *Linear Regression* class, which must be imported from Scikit-Learn. The import can be done as follows:

```
from sklearn.linear_model import LinearRegression
```

Now that we have imported the class, we need to instantiate it and give the instance the name

linear_regressor. This is demonstrated below:

```
linear_regressor = LinearRegression()
```

Let us now call the *fit()* method and pass the training data to it:

```
linear_regressor.fit(X_train, y_train)
```

As we had stated earlier, Linear Regression works by finding the best values for the slope and the intercept. This is what we have done above. These two have been calculated, so we only have to view their values.

To see the intercept, run the following command:

print(linear_regressor.intercept_) Predicting

In the training done above, we have created a linear regression model, which is the equation. The values for the slope and the intercept are known. We can make predictions based on the data we preserved as the training set. The following statement helps us make predictions from the test data:

```
pred_y = linear_regressor.predict(X_test)
```

We have simply created a NumPy array named *predict_y*. This will have all the predicted values for y from the input values contained in the *X_test* series. We now have the actual values for the X_test as well as the predicted values. We need to compare these two and see the amount of similarity or difference between the two. Just run the following code:

```
df = pd.Data Frame ({'Actual': y_test, 'Predicted': pred_y}) print(df)
```

The model is not accurate, but the values are close to each other.

Evaluating the Accuracy

We now need to evaluate the accuracy of our algorithm. We need to determine how well the algorithm performed on the dataset. When it comes to regression algorithms, three evaluation metrics are used. These include the following:

1. Mean Absolute Error.

2. Mean Square Error.

3. Root Mean Squared Error.

Multiple Linear Regression

You now know how to do a Linear Regression when you have two variables. However, this is not a true reflection of what we have in the real world. Most of the problems the world is facing involve more than two variables. This explains why you need to learn Multiple Linear Regression. The steps between the two are almost the same. However, the difference comes when it comes to evaluation. When evaluating the multiple linear regression model, we need to know the factor with the highest impact on the output variable. We also need to determine the relationship between the various variables.

We need to demonstrate this by prediction the consumption of fuel in US states. We will consider factors like per capita income, gas taxes, paved highways, and the proportion of persons who have a driver's license.

Let us first import the libraries that we need to use:

```
import numpy as np
import pandas as pd
import matplotlib.pyplot as plt
```

Again, you may get an error for trying to print the contents of the dataset. Use the method we used previously to solve the problem. You should have the following code:

```
import numpy as np
import pandas as pd
import matplotlib.pyplot as plt
import sys
sys.__stdout__ = sys.stdout
dataset = pd.read_csv('fuel_consumption.csv')
print(dataset.head())
```

Data Preparation

In the example of simple linear regression, we subdivided the data into attributes and labels. In this case, we will be directly using the column names for this purpose. Run the code given below:

```
X = dataset[['Tax', 'Income', 'Highways',
'Licence']]
y = dataset['Consumption']
```

We have four columns for the attributes (the independent variables) and one column for the label (the dependent variable). Let us now subdivide the data into training and test sets. 80% of the data will be used as the training set while the remaining 20% will be used as the test set:

First, let us import the *train_test_split()* method from Scikit-Learn:

from sklearn.model_selection import train_test_split

Run the following command to do the division of the data:

X_train, X_test, y_train, y_test = train_test_split(X, y, test_size=0.2, random_state=0)

Training the Algorithm

We now need to train the algorithm. This can be done by calling the *fit()* method, as we did previously. Let us first import the Linear Regression class from the Scikit-Learn library:

from sklearn.linear_model import LinearRegression

Next, create an instance of the above class then use it to call the *fit()* method:
linear_regressor = LinearRegression()

linear_regressor.fit(X_train, y_train)

Note that this is a multiple linear regression and we have many variables. The linear regression model has to find the optimal coefficients for each attribute. You can see the chosen coefficients by running the following command:

```
coeff = pd.Data Frame (linear_regressor.coef_, X.columns, columns=['Coefficient'])
print(coeff)
```

```
             Coefficient
Tax          -40.016660
Income        -0.065413
Highways      -0.004741
Licence     1341.862121
```

This means that any unit increase in fuel tax will lead to a decrease of 40.02 million gallons in gas Consumption. Also, a unit increase in the proportion of the population with Driver's license will lead to an increase of 1.342 billion gallons in gas Consumption. The results also show that average Income and Highways have a very small impact on gas Consumption.

Predicting

We will make the predictions using the test data. The following script can help us do this: pred_y = linear_regressor.predict(X_test)

At this point, you have the actual X_text values as well as the predicted values. We need to perform a comparison between these two to determine their similarities and differences. This can be done by running the following script:

df = pd.Data Frame ({'Actual': y_test, 'Predicted': pred_y}) print(df)

Evaluating the Accuracy

We now need to evaluate the algorithm in terms of performance. This can be done by determining the values for the various types of errors. These include the MAE, RMSE, and MSE. This requires us to firm import the *metrics* class from Scikit-Learn:

from sklearn import metrics

The calculation of the error values can then be done using the following script:

```
print('MAE:', metrics.mean_absolute_error(y_test, pred_y))
print('MSE:', metrics.mean_squared_error(y_test, pred_y))
print('RMSE:', np.sqrt(metrics.mean_squared_error(y_test, pred_y)))
```

The value for the root means the square error is 68.31, as shown above. This is slightly greater than 10% of the mean value for gas consumption in all the states. It is true that our algorithm was not very much accurate, but we can still use it to make predictions. The big error could be brought by a number of factors. Maybe there was a need for more data. We have used data for only one year. Having data collected over multiple years could have helped us improve the accuracy of the model. Also, we had assumed that our data has a linear relationship. This could not be the case, hence the big error. I recommend that you visualize the data to see whether this is true. Also, the features we have used could not be correlated.

CHAPTER SEVEN

THE BASICS OF HACKING

Hacking is nothing but unauthorized intrusion within a network or computer which is executed by attackers known as hackers. The attackers try to attack those systems which are vulnerable to threats. They keep their prying eyes open all the time, searching around for vulnerabilities. They can act as an individual or even work in a group. Not only might that but the hackers also function as a part of an organization which works with the motive of disrupting the functionalities of other organizations. Most of the time they try to alter the system of an organization and target the security infrastructure for breaching of information and gaining access. However, hackers not only work as attackers but also use their skills for finding out the weak spots along with the various vulnerabilities within a system. This is also carried out for finding and mending the weaknesses for preventing all forms of malicious attacks from entering the system.

Different Types of Hackers

There are various types of hackers in the world of hacking which perform different types of functions. The types of hackers help in defining the relationship between the systems and hackers which are trying to attack. The most common types of hackers are:

1. Black Hat Hackers

The term black hat had its origin from the old Western movies in which the villains used to wear black hats. The black hat hackers act as individuals who try to have unauthorized access into the system of an organization or network for the purpose of exploiting the security infrastructure for various malicious reasons. The hackers of this type do not come with any sort of authority or permission for compromising the targets. They attempt to do damage by compromising the infrastructure of the security systems, shutting down the systems or also by altering the primary functions of a website or network. The primary intention of the black hat hackers is to gain all-over access or steal the information regarding finances, access various passwords or gain insights into other forms of personal data.

2. White Hat Hackers

The white hat hackers are the second type of hackers but they act as the good guys. The white hat hackers work with various organizations for the purpose of strengthening the security of any system. The white hat hackers come with all sorts of permissions for engaging the targets and also compromise the same within the provided boundary of rules. The white hat hackers are also known as ethical hackers. The ethical hackers specialize in this field with various forms of ethical tools and techniques meant for hacking. They use special methodologies for securing up the information system of an organization. Contrary to the black hat hackers, the ethical hackers exploit the security system of a network and then check out for the backdoors after being legally permitted to perform so. The ethical hackers always point out all forms of vulnerabilities that they dig out from the systems of the organizations to make sure that the gaps are mended for preventing exploitation by the malicious attackers.

3. Grey Hat Hackers

The grey hat hackers gain access to the security systems of the organizations and networks in the same way just like black hat hackers do. But the grey hat hackers perform such actions without any form of malicious intent and disclose the vulnerabilities along with the loopholes to the agencies of law enforcement or various intelligence agencies. The grey hat hackers generally surf the internet and hack the computer systems for notifying the owners or the administrator of the network or system which contains various vulnerabilities which need to be mended immediately. The grey hat hackers might also extort the hacked systems by offering to inform about the defects for some fees too.

Common Tools of Hacking

For accomplishing the act of hacking, the hackers implement various types of techniques. Let's have a look at some of them.

1. Rootkits

Rootkit acts like a program or a huge set of software which allows the attackers to gain complete access or control of a system or network which directly connects or interacts with the system of the internet. Rootkit was first introduced as a system of backdoor process for fixing various issues in regards to software. However, today this software is widely being used by the hackers for disrupting the functionality and control of a system from its actual owner or administrators. There are various ways in which rootkits can be installed in the system of the victim. The most common way of installing rootkit is by implementing phishing attacks along with social engineering. Once the rootkits have been installed in the system of the victim, the attacker gains access to the system secretly and controls the overall functioning with which they can easily steal confidential data and information and can also shut down a system completely.

2. Keyloggers

This is a very special type of tool which has been designed for recording and logging each and every key pressed on the victim system. The keyloggers record the stroke of the keys by staying attached to the Application Programming Interface or API. It tracks the key strokes when anything is being typed by using the keyboard in a system. The files which are recorded are then saved which contains various forms of information such as details regarding website visit, usernames, the record of opened applications, screenshots, bank details and many more. The keyloggers are also capable of capturing the personal messages, credit card details, passwords, mobile numbers and various other details which are generally typed in a system. The keyloggers generally arrive as a malware which allows the cybercriminals to breach all forms of sensitive data.

3. Vulnerability scanner

A vulnerability scanner is used for the purpose of classifying and then detecting various forms of weaknesses in a system, network, communication system, computers etc. This is one of the most common forms of tool which is being used by the ethical hackers for finding out the potential vulnerabilities and loopholes and then fixes them up on urgent basis. However, a vulnerability scanner can also be used by the black hat hackers for checking the vulnerabilities and weak spots within a system and then finding out the proper tool for exploiting the same.

Techniques of Hacking

There are various techniques which are being used by the hackers for exploiting a system.

1. SQL Injection

SQL or structured query language has been designed for the purpose of exploiting various forms of data in the database of the victim. This form of attack falls under the cyber-attack which targets the databases via the statements of SQL for tricking the systems. This form of attack is generally carried out by the use of website interface which attempts in issuing the commands of SQL through a database for hacking the passwords, usernames and other related information related to the database. All those websites along with web applications which are coded poorly are very much prone to the SQL injection attacks. This is because the applications which are based on the web contains various user input fields like login pages, search pages, request forms related to support and products, comments section and many others which are very much susceptible to the attacks and can be very easily hacked by simple manipulation of the codes.

2. DDoS or Distributed Denial of Service

It is a form of hacking attack in which the normal traffic of a server is distorted from entering the server and floods the traffic of the network. This ultimately results in denial of service as it serves just like a traffic jam which clogs the roads and also prevents the regular form of traffic from reaching the destination. All the devices of today such as IoT devices, computers, mobile phones etc. which connects with the network are very much prone to the attacks of DDoS.

3. MAC Spoofing

Each and every form of device which are used by the people today come with network interface controller or NIC. It helps the users to connect with the network such as with the internet directly. The NIC of each device is accompanied with a MAC address which is assigned after various processes of hard coding. The MAC spoofing attack is a very deadly form of attack in which the hackers hide themselves and their system behind a customized and false MAC address. This reduces the risks on the part of the hackers from getting caught. So, you might give access to a new system thinking of it to be absolutely legitimate but it might happen that a hacker will hide himself behind a false MAC address which you cannot even realize.

By using this technique, the hackers can easily hack internet connection via Wi-Fi and can also gain access to all those devices which are connected to each other via LAN. The technique of MAC spoofing also leads to several forms of other serious crimes in which the hackers steal the identity of someone else and carries on with some serious form of data breaching in which someone will be held as guilty without even knowing about the actual hacker. However, there are various OS in the market today such as MAC and Windows which can easily connect with the LAN without using the MAC address.

CHAPTER EIGHT

ETHICAL HACKING

Ethical hacking is also called as intrusion testing, penetration testing and also red teaming. In simple words, it is the controversial technique of finding out vulnerabilities and weaknesses in a system simply by imitating the actions and intent of the malicious hackers. An ethical hacker is a person or security professional who uses his skills for the purpose of various defensive measures on part of the administrators of an information system. An ethical hacker is also known as a white hat or white hat hacker. By conducting various tests, an ethical hacker tries to find out the answers to the following questions:

1. What are the locations, systems or information can the attacker gain access?
2. What will the attacker see before setting his target?
3. What will the attacker do with the information which is available in the system?
4. Is anyone able to notice the various attempts made by the attacker to gain access?

The ethical hacker who has been given the job of penetration testing operates on the permission along with the knowledge of that organization for which he has been assigned the job of defense. There are various cases in which an organization will not be informing the security information team about all the activities which is going to be carried out by the ethical hacker just for testing the effectiveness and concise of the security information team. This whole thing is also known as

double blind environment. For the purpose of effective and legal operation, the organization needs to inform an ethical hacker about all those assets and information which are meant to be protected, the potential sources of threats and the limit to which the organization will be supporting the efforts of the ethical hacker.

The Process of ethical hacking

All the ethical hackers follow a strict process in order to get the best usable and to the point legal results. Let's have a look at the processes which are followed by the ethical hackers.

1. Planning

No matter what kind of project it is, for every successful project planning is of utmost importance. It provides the ethical hackers with the opportunity of thinking about what are the things that need to be done, set the goals which are to be reached and also for the assessments of risks for evaluating how to carry out a complete project. There are various factors which are considered by the ethical hackers before carrying out a project of ethical hacking. The list of factors includes culture, policies of security, laws, regulations, requirements of the industry and best practices. All of these factors play an important role in the process of decision making when it comes to the initiation of ethical hacking.

The phase of planning in ethical hacking will be having an overall influence on how the process of hacking is being performed, the information which is collected and shared and will also be directly influencing the integration and delivery of the results into the program of security. The planning phase is the very first step and will be describing most of the details about the controlled attack of hacking. It will also be answering all forms of questions regarding hacking such as how the process of ethical hacking is going to be controlled and supported, what are the basic actions which needs to be performed and for how long will the process go on.

2. Reconnaissance

It is the process of searching for all those information which are freely available for assisting in the process of attack. This whole process can be as easy and simple as just using a ping or browsing the various newsgroups which are available on the internet for searching that information which is leaked by the employees or as tough and messy as digging through a huge trash of letter or receipts. This process can also include several other processes such as phone tapping, social engineering, network tapping and also data theft. The process of information searching will be limited only to the extent to which the organization and the ethical hacker will want to go for the purpose of recovering all the required information which they are looking out for.

The phase of reconnaissance introduces the deep relationship in between the tasks which needs to be completed and all those methods which will be needed for protecting the information and assets of the organization.

3. Enumeration

It is also known as vulnerability or network discovery. Enumeration is the process of obtaining all those information which is available readily from the system of the target, networks and application which are used by the target. It is also to be noted that the phase of enumeration is the actual point where the thin line between malicious attacks and ethical hacking gets blurred very often as it is very easy and simple to go outside the dedicated boundaries which have been outlined in the original plan of attack. For the purpose of creating a clear picture of the environment of an organization, various techniques and tools are being used which are readily available. These available tools include NMap and port scanning. However, it is very easy to collect all the required information, it is very difficult to make sure of the value of information which is available in the hands of the hacker.

At the very first glance, the process of enumeration seems to be very simple in which data is collected then evaluated collectively for establishing a proper plan for more searching or building up a detailed matrix for the analysis or vulnerability phase. However, this phase is the actual phase in which the ability of ethical hacker in taking logical decisions plays a very important role.

4. Analysis of vulnerability

For the purpose of effectively analyzing all the data, an ethical hacker needs to employ a pragmatic approach which is logical in nature as well. In the phase of vulnerability analysis, all the information which has been collected is compared with all the known forms of vulnerabilities in the practical process. Any form of information is useful in the process, no matter from where it originates or what the source is. A small pinch of information can also help in finding out some new sort of vulnerability in the system and might also lead to several other discoveries of vulnerabilities which have not been found yet. The known form of vulnerabilities, service packs, incidents, updates along with various hacker tools helps in properly identifying the point of attack. The internet provides the ethical hackers with a huge amount of information which can be associated very easily with the system architecture along with weak and strong points in a system.

5. Exploitation

A considerable amount of time is spent for the purpose of evaluating and planning an ethical hack. It is very obvious that all of these planning will lead to some sort of attack. The level of exploitation of a system can be as simple as running a very small tool in the system or as tough as a collection of many complex steps which needs to be executed in a proper way for gaining access to the system. The process of exploitation can be broken into a collection of subtasks which can be either one single step or a collection of various steps. As each and every step is performed, a process of evaluation takes place which ensures that the outcome which has been expected is met. Any form of divergence from the plan of attack can be graded into two parts:

- **Expectation:** Are the expected results of exploitation met or the results are conflicting with the assumptions of the organization?
- **Technical:** Is the target system behaving in a manner which is not at all expected, which is actually having an impact on the system exploitation and the system engagement in total?

Final analysis

Although the phase of exploitation comes with a huge number of validations and checks for ensuring the success of the hack, one last final analysis is needed for categorizing the system vulnerabilities in accordance to the exposure level and also for assisting in the drawing up of a plan for mitigation. The phase of final analysis links up the exploitation phase and the deliverable creation. A comprehensive image of the complete attack is needed for the construction of a bigger size picture of the current posture of the security environment of an organization and also for expressing the vulnerabilities clearly.

Deliverables

Deliverable communicates with the test results in a variety of ways. Some of the deliverables are concise and short in nature which only provides the vulnerabilities list along with the ways in which it can be mended whereas, the other form of deliverables can be detailed and long which will provide a list of the probable vulnerabilities in a system which comes with the description regarding how the vulnerabilities were found, how they can be exploited, the results of having such vulnerabilities within the system and how to fix the situation. This phase is actually used by an ethical hacker in conveying his hack results to the organization. It can also be the case if the deliverables do not actually frighten the administrators, the test is considered as a fail.

CHAPTER NINE

CYBER SECURITY

In this world of today where technological innovations are taking place every day, the potential threats of cyber-attacks are also increasing in equal pace. Cyber security plays a deep role in securing the information and data of the systems and networks in today's world of vulnerability. Cyber security is nothing but the employment of various tools and technologies for the purpose of securing the networks, programs, system data and network from the potential attacks, damages and various forms of unauthorized access. Cyber security is also known as security of information technology.

Cyber security and its importance

Most of the organizations and institutions such as military, government, medical along with financial bodies stores up an accountable amount of data on the systems of computers along with databases which can be found online. In most of the cases, the information which is being stored up in the servers and databases are highly sensitive in nature, leakage of which can result in serious troubles for the concerned organization. Unauthorized access to the systems of the organizations along with the database can lead to data breaching along with the exploitation of the security infrastructure of an organization.

The organizations which are targeted might lose up all forms of sensitive data along with complete loss of access to the systems. As the volume of cyber-attacks is increasing day by day, the organizations especially those which are concerned with national health and security are required to take some serious steps for safeguarding all forms of sensitive data. Cyber security is the ultimate option which can help an organization in protecting all its data and servers.

Cyber Security & Encryption

Encryption is the process of encoding communication in such a way so that only the authorized parties can encode the message of communication. It is done by using SSL/TLS and PKI protocols. The very reason why is it important so much stems from the process in which the internet was built up by using the protocol of HTTP. Hypertext Transfer Protocol or HTTP is of the same age that of the internet. HTTP is the protocol of communication which allows the servers in the web and the web browsers for communicating and displaying the information in a proper intended way. When a user visits a website, it is not actually the way it looks in the browser. Websites are built up of a bunch of codes which are sent to the web browsers which are then visually arranged by the browser in the way the web designer intended to do.

The main problem of HTTP is that it is not at all secure. So, any person who knows the process can easily spy on the connections of HTTP on the internet. In simple words, a third party can easily read along with manipulate a communication over

HTTP between the clients and the servers. Encryption is the technique that actually comes into play in taking care of the communication by serving the websites over the protocol of HTTPS. HTTPS is the secured version of HTTP. All the connections which are built over HTTPS are encrypted in nature. In simple terms, any form of communication over the protocol of HTTPS is highly secure. Encryption prevents spying on communication by the third parties. In case you are related with online business and you need to take the financial as well as personal details of the customers, make sure that your website is encrypted so that your customers are not at risk at the time of details exchange.

How does the process of encryption work?

The process of encryption begins when the web browser reaches one website which comes with an SSL certificate. The web server and the browser proceeds with what is known as SSL handshake. At the preliminary stages, the web browser verifies that the SSL certificate which is installed in the website is legitimate in nature and has been issued by a trustworthy authority of certification. After the web browser makes sure that the certificate is legitimate in nature, it starts to negotiate with the terms of the encrypted connection with the server.

When it comes to encryption, there are mainly two key pairs. The first is the asymmetric key pair which consists of the private and public keys. These keys have no function with the encryption bulk but they are used for authentication. When a web browser tests the authenticity of SSL certificate of a website, it makes sure that the certificate of SSL which is being questioned is actually the owner of the public form of key. It performs this by using up the public key for encrypting a small packet of data. If the web server is able to decrypt the data packet by using the respective private key and then send the packet back, it is proved that the server is the owner of the public key and everything is stated as verified. In case the web server fails to decrypt the data packet, the certificate of the server is taken as "not trusted".

The other key pair is the session keys. This form of keys is generated after the authenticity of the SSL certificate has been verified and all the terms regarding encryption have also been negotiated. While a public key can be used only for encrypting and a private key for decrypting, the session keys can be used for both the functions of encryption and decryption. The session keys are smaller in size and also less secure in nature when compared with the asymmetric form of counterparts. However, the session keys are strong enough for performing both the functions. The server and the web browser use the session keys for the rest of the communication. After leaving the site, the session keys which are being used are discarded and brand-new session keys are generated for the new visit.

Common Types of Cyber Attacks

Cyber-attacks are increasing day by day with the innovations in the world of technology. There are various types of cyber-attacks that can be found today where some are used most commonly such as phishing, malware, XSS and many more. Let's have a look at some of the most common types of cyber-attacks.

1. Malware

Malware is a form of harmful software which is used for gaining access to the systems of the victims. The malware can also be called as viruses. Once a malware enters the victim system, it can lead to havoc starting from gaining overall control of the system to the monitoring of all sorts of actions, stealing sensitive data silently and also can lead to a complete shutdown of the system. The attackers use various ways for inserting malware in the target system. But there are also various cases in which the system users are being tricked into installing a malware in the system.

2. Phishing

Receiving emails with various unwanted links and attachments is a very common thing today. Such action of sending out harmful links and attachments via email is known as phishing. In phishing attacks, the attackers send out emails to the targets which seem like a trustable email. Most of the emails come with links and attachments which when clicked leads to the installation of malware in the system without even the user of the system knowing nothing. Some of the phishing links can also lead the users to a new website which might ask for confidential data such as bank and credit card details. Such websites are actually a trap which is used by the attackers for installing the malware in the target systems.

3. XSS

Cross-site scripting or XSS attack is used for targeting the users of a website directly. It is somewhat similar to the SQL injection attack and also involves injecting harmful codes in a website. But, in the case of XSS attacks, the websites are not attacked. In an XSS attack, the malicious code which has been injected in the website runs only in the browser of the user and can be used for stealing sensitive data such as username, password, bank details and many more.

Malware and Its Types

Malware is a form of malicious software which is being used for gaining access to the system of the victim. The cyber criminals design malware in a way which can be used for stealing data, compromising the functions of the computer, bypassing the access controls and many more.

Types of malwares

There are various types of malwares that can be found today. Let's have a look at them.

1. Adware

Adware are those programs which are used for displaying advertisements on the websites which when clicked redirects to the website which is being advertised and also collects all forms of market data about the user. There are also various forms of pop-up adware that generally contains malicious links which can lead to harm of the system.

2. Spyware

It is a software which is used for spying the target users. It has been designed for capturing and monitoring the activities of the users on the websites. Adware is also a form of spyware which sends out the activities of browsing of the users to the advertisers.

3. Worm

Worm is a form of virus which is being used by the cybercriminals for the purpose of replicating themselves. Worms use computer networks for spreading and can lead to stealing or deletion of data. Many of the worms are also being designed for spreading only through the systems and do not lead to any form of harm to the systems.

CHAPTER TEN

LINUX ARCHITECTURE

L inux is one of the finest operating systems which can be found today. It is open source in nature and is based on UNIX. It is just a simple OS like the commercial ones like Windows XP, Windows 10 and MAC OS. An OS is nothing but the graphical form of interface between the system of a computer and the user of the system. It comes with the responsibility of managing all the resources related to hardware that the system of a computer has and also helps in establishing communication in between the hardware and the software.

Open-Source Software

An open-source software is a software which has its source code available with the license with which the holder of copyright has the right to study the software, change the settings and also distribute the same software with anyone he wants for any form of purpose.

Linux OS and its components

The Linux OS is composed of three different components.

1. The Kernel
2. The System Library

3. The System Utility

1. The Kernel

The kernel functions as the core part of any form of OS. It is responsible for handling the tasks along with the hardware of the system of a computer. The CPU time and memory are the two examples of the entities which are being managed by the kernel. The kernel of an OS is of two types:

. Microkernel

The microkernel is a type of OS kernel. As its name goes by, it comes with a very basic form of functionality. It is the least amount of software which can provide with the environment which is required for the functioning of an operating system. This environment of kernel covers management of threads, low level management of address space and inter-process form of communication.

. Monolithic kernel

Monolithic kernel is the form of kernel which comes with various drivers along with it. It is an architecture of the operating system in which the operating system of a system works in the space of kernel. This form of the kernel is able to load or unload dynamically all the modules which are executable at the time of running. The monolithic form of kernel stays in the supervisor mode. The major point of difference between the micro kernel and the monolithic kernel is that the monolithic form of kernel can alone define a very high level of interface over the hardware of the system of a computer.

Supervisor mode

The supervisor mode of the monolithic kernel is a flag which mediates from the hardware of a system. It can be easily modified by running the codes in the software system level. All form of system level tasks comes with this flag while they are operating or running. However, the applications of user space do not come with this flag set. The flag makes sure that whether the execution of machine code operations is possible or not such as performing various operations like disabling the interruptions or modifying the registers for various forms of descriptor table. The main idea behind having two different types of operation comes from the idea "with more amount of control come more responsibilities"

Any program in the supervisor mode is trusted so much that it will never fail as any form of failure will lead to crashing of the computer system. In simple words, the kernel is the component which is responsible for all form of activities of the OS. It is composed of various types of modules and also directly interacts with the base hardware. The kernel comes with all the necessary abstraction for the purpose of hiding all the low-level details of hardware to system or programs of application.

2. The System Library

The system library is composed of a collection of resources which are non-volatile in nature and are used up by the resources of the computer system and is mainly used for developing software. This comes with data configuration, help data, documentation, templates for messaging and many more. Generally, the term library is being used for describing a huge collection of implementations regarding behavior which is written down in terms of computer language. It comes with a perfectly defined form of interface which helps in invoking the behavior. So, this means that anyone who wants to create a program of high level can easily use up the system library for the purpose of making system calls continuously.

The system library can be requested at a time by various individual forms of programs simultaneously, in order to make sure that the library has been coded in a way so that several programs can use up the library even when the concerned programs are not at all linked nor have a connection with each other. In simple terms, the system libraries are unique programs or form of functions built up of the system utilities or application programs which have access to all the features of the kernel. This form of library implements a majority of the functions related to the operating system of a computer and they are not required to have the rights of code access for the module of the kernel.

3. The System Utility

The programs of system utility are responsible for performing all forms of individual and specialized level tasks. The utility software is a form of system software. It has been designed for running the programs of application and hardware for a system of computer. The system software can also be considered as the interface between the applications of the users and the hardware. In simple words, the system utility software is the software of a system which has been designed for the purpose of configuring, analyzing, optimizing and maintaining a system of computer. The utility software works hand in hand with the operating system for supporting the infrastructure of a system, differentiating it from the software of application which is aimed for performing the various tasks directly which will be benefiting the normal users.

Characteristics of Linux architecture

Linux comes with various features that can help the regular users a lot.

1. Multiuser capability

This is the most unique characteristic of Linux OS in which the resources of a computer such as memory, hard disk etc. can be accessed by various users at a time. However, the users access the resources not from a single terminal. Each of the users is given an individual terminal for accessing the resources and operating them. A terminal consists of at least one VDU, mouse and keyboard as the devices for input. All the terminals are linked or connected with the primary server or Linux or with the host machine the resources of which and other peripheral devices like printer can be used by the users.

2. Multitasking

Linux OS comes with the capability of easily handling various jobs at a time. For example, a user can execute a command for the purpose of execution of a huge list and type in a notepad at the same time. This is intelligently managed by dividing the time of CPU by implementing the policies of scheduling along with the concept of switching of contexts.

3. Portability

Portability is the feature that made Linux OS so famous among the users. Portability does not mean at all that it can be carried around in CDs, pen drive or memory cars nor the size of the file is small. By portability, it means that the OS of Linux along with all its application can function on various types of hardware in the exact same way. The kernel of Linux and the application programs of the OS support the installation of the same on even those systems which comes with the least configuration of hardware.

4. Security

Security is considered as the most essential part of any operating system. It is really important for all those users and organizations who are using the system for various forms of confidential tasks. Linux OS comes with various concepts of security for the purpose of protecting the users from any form of unauthorized access of the system and their data.

The Main concepts of Linux security

Linux provides 3 main types of security concepts.

1. Authentication

This helps in authenticating the user with the system by providing login names and password for the individual users so that their work cannot be accessed by any third party.

2. Authorization

At the file level of Linux OS, it comes with limits of authorization for the users. There are write, read and execution permissions for every file which determines who all can access the files, who can modify the same and who all can execute the files.

3. Encryption

This feature of Linux OS helps in encoding the user files into a format which is unreadable in format and is called cyphertext. This makes sure that even if someone becomes successful in opening up the system, the files will be safe.

Communication

Linux OS comes with a great feature for the purpose of communicating with the users. It can be either within the network of one single computer or in between two or more than two networks of a computer. The users of such systems can seamlessly exchange data, mail and programs through the networks.

CHAPTER ELEVEN

THE BASICS OF LINUX OPERATING SYSTEM

Linux is a simple operating system just like other operating systems such as Windows. As an OS, Linux helps in managing the hardware of a system and also provides services that the other software needs for running. It is regarded as a hands-on operating system. For example, if running an OS like Windows is like an automatic car, running Linux OS is like driving a stick. It might need some more work to do, but once the user gets a nice grip of the functioning of Linux, using the line of commands and also installing the packages will become super easy.

The History of Linux

Linux is similar to the MAC OS X, which is also based on Unix. Unix was developed in the early 1970s with a primary goal of creating an OS which will turn out to be accessible and also secure at the same time for various users. In 1991, Linux was developed with the goal of distributing the features of Unix. It was launched as open-source software and till date, it is the same. Open-source software is a software whose code is visible completely by the user and can also be modified according to need and can be redistributed. Linux is just the kernel and not a complete OS. The kernel provides for an interface between the hardware and requests from the user applications. The other part of the OS consists of utilities, GNU libraries and various other software. The OS as one complete unit is called as GNU/Linux.

A bit of servers

The Linode that the users have is a type of server. A server is nothing but a type of master computer which helps in providing various forms of service all over the network or across a connected network of computers. The servers are generally:

- Stays on all the time.
- It is generally connected with the internet or a group of computer networks.
- Consists of files and programs for the purpose of website hosting or for other content of the Internet.

As the server acts just like a computer, there are various similarities in between the Linode and the home computer. Some of the similarities are:

- The Linode is generally hosted on a physical form of machine. It sits on the available pool of data centers.
- Linodes uses up OS like Linux. It is another type of OS similar to Mac or Windows. Just like a user can easily install various applications in their PC, applications can be installed on Linode as well. All these applications which are installed on a Linode help in performing various tasks like hosting a website.
- A user can easily create, edit and delete files just like it can be done on a PC. The user can navigate through the directories as well just like PC.

- Just like a PC, Linodes are connected with the internet.

Things to consider before installing Linux

Before installing Linux, you need to make sure which distribution of Linux you want to install. Linux OS comes in various versions which are known as distributions. The distributions are similar to that of the versions of OS like Windows 7 or Windows XP. The new versions of operating systems like Windows are the upgraded versions. But, in case of Linux, the distributions are not upgraded but are of various flavors. Several distributions of Linux install various different software bundles.

Linux Distributions

The major difference between the distributions of Linux tends to be from the aspect of aims and goals of the distribution and which software bundles are installed rather than any form of difference in the Linux kernel code. RedHat Linux which consists of CentOS and Fedora and Debian Linux which consists of Ubuntu shares a huge number of codes with one another. The kernels are more or less the same and the applications along with user utilities from the project of GNU are also similar. Some of the distributions of Linux have been designed to be as minimalistic and simple as possible whereas some has been designed having the current and the best software of the era. All the distributions of Linux aim at providing the best stability and reliability to the users.

In addition to the individual personality of distributions, you will also need to consider various factors which will help you at the time of choosing your desired distribution.

1. Release cycle

The various distributions of Linux release the updates of their OS at different schedules. The distributions like Arch Linux and Gentoo uses a model of rolling release in which each individual package is released when they are declared as complete or ready by the developers. Distributions like Slackware, Debian and CentOS targets in providing the users with the most stable form of operating system which will be attainable as well and also releases the newer versions very frequently. Linux distributions such as Ubuntu and Fedora release its new versions after every six months. Selecting the release cycle which will be perfect for you also depends on various factors. The factors include the software that you require to run, the amount of reliability and stability that you require and the comfort level you are looking out for.

2. Organizational structure

Although it might not directly affect the distribution performance, it is still one of the most distinguishing factors in between the Linux distributions. Some of the Linux distributions like Gentoo, Debian, Slackware and Arch are all developed by the communities of independent developers while some of the other distributions such as Ubuntu, Fedora and OpenSUSE are developed by those communities which are being sponsored by different corporations. Distribution like CentOS is derived from the distributions which are produced commercially.

3. Common set of tools

The various distributions of Linux use different types of tools for performing various common tasks such as configuration of system or management of packages. Distributions like Ubuntu and Debian uses APT for managing the .deb packages, OpenSUSE uses .rpm package and CentOS along with Fedora also uses .rpm packages but manages all of them by using a tool known as yast. In most of the cases the distribution you choose will end up to that one distribution which comes with all the tools which you require and you are comfortable with.

The distributions are designed for performing in different situations. You are required to start with experimenting the distributions for finding out the one that fits you the best according to your need.

Linux security

When you start using a system based on Linux OS, you become the owner of your system security. The internet is filled up with people who are waiting to use the computing power of your system for satisfying their own goals. Linux offers the users with various security options that help the users in securing their system and tuning the same according to their need.

1. Finding your folders and files

Everything on a Linux system is in the form of a directory. In Linux, a folder is termed as a directory. Linux OS uses a well-balanced tree of various nested directories for keeping all the files in an organized manner. The directory of the highest level is known as the root directory. It comes designated with only one single slash. In Windows OS, you will come across various drives and disks. But this is not the case in Linux OS. There are several other sub-directories which lie under the root directory. Most of the systems based on Linux come with directories which are called as var and lib along with many others under the tree of the root directory. The directory of lib consists of the system libraries whereas the directory of var consists of all sorts of files which are available in the system which are most likely to change like the mail messages and logs. The directories of Linux OS can also go inside the other directories.

2. Users and permissions

Linux OS uses a very powerful system for the users and its permissions for making sure that only the right people get access to the system files. As the owner of your Linux system, you can set the users and permissions for every directory. The file access system in Linux comprises of three categories.

Users: A user account is assigned generally to a person or also to an application which requires access to the files in the system. You can provide user access to the system as many numbers you want.

Groups: A group is the collection of one or more than one user. Groups are a great way of granting the same kind of access to various users at one time without the need for setting permissions for each individually. When you create an account of user, it gets assigned to a default group which comes with the same name as that of the name of the user. A user can be a part of as many groups as the user wants. Users who belong to a group get all the permissions which are granted for that specific group.

Everyone: This category is for everyone other than the groups and users. When someone accesses the system files without even logging in the system as one specific user, they fall into the category of everyone.

The next important thing that comes right after users is permissions. Each and every directory and file in a Linux system comes with three probable levels of access.

- **Read:** All the files that come with the permission of read can be viewed.
- **Write:** All the files that come with the permission of write can be edited.
- **Execute:** All the files that come with the permission of execute can be executed or run just like an application. When you start a new script or program, you start executing it.

Software installation in Linux

Like all the other things in the Linux system, software installation is also done by typing and then executing one specific form of text command. Most of the distributions in Linux come along with managers of package which makes it easier for installing or uninstalling any software in the system. Distributions such as Ubuntu and Debian use APT or the Advanced Packaging Tool package manager whereas CentOS and Fedora use YUM or Yellowdog Updater Modified manager of packages.

CHAPTER TWELVE

KALIX LINUX AND ITS IMPORTANCE IN THE HACKING WORLD

Kali Linux is a distribution of Linux which is based on Debian. It has been designed very significantly for the purpose of catering to the needs of the network analysts along with the penetration testers. The wide range of tools that come along with Kali Linux makes it the prime weapon of all the ethical hackers. Kali Linux was previously called Backtrack. Kali Linux is the successor of Backtrack with a more polished version of tools than Backtrack which used to serve the same purpose with a wide range of tools and making the OS jam-packed with several utilities which were not at all necessary. That is why the ethical hackers turned towards Kali Linux which provides tools required for penetration testing in a more simplified form for the ease of functioning.

Why this OS?

Kali Linux comes with a plethora of features. There are also various reasons that justify why one start using Kali Linux should.

1. **Free of cost:** Linux is a free software and so all the distributions of Linux are also free of cost. Kali Linux has been and will also be free of cost always.

2. **A wide array of tools:** Kali Linux can offer you with more than 600 different types of tools for penetration testing and also various tools related to security analysis.

3. **Open-source software:** Linux is an open-source software. So, Kali Linux being a part of the Linux family also follows the much-appreciated model of being open-source. The tree of development of the OS can be viewed publicly on Git and all the codes which are available with Kali Linux are also available for the purpose of tweaking.

4. **Support for multi-language:** Although of the fact that the penetration tools are written in English, it is evident that Kali Linux supports multilingual use as well. It has been done to make sure that a greater number of users can operate the OS in their native language and can also locate the tools which they need for their job.

5. **Totally customizable:** The developers of the tools for offensive security know that every user will not be agreeing with the model design. So, Kali Linux has been developed in a way so that it can be fully customized according to the need and liking of the user.

System requirements

Installing Kali Linux for the purpose of penetration testing is very easy. You just need to make sure that you have the required set of hardware. Kali Linux is supported on amd64, i386 and ARM. You all require:

- Minimum 20 GB of disk space for the installation of the software
- Minimum 1 GB of RAM
- One CD/DVD drive or virtual box

List of tools

Kali Linux comes with a wide range of tools pre-installed. Let's have a look at some of the most commonly used tools.

1. Air crack-ng

It is a tools suite which is used for the purpose of assessing Wi-Fi network security. It aims at some of the prime areas of security related to Wi-Fi.

- **Monitoring:** It helps in capturing packet and also exports data to the text files for processing in the later stages by the third-party tools.
- **Attacking:** It helps in replay attacks, fake access points, de-authentication and various others by the process of packet injection.
- **Testing:** It helps in checking the Wi-Fi cards and other capabilities of the drivers.

- **Cracking:** It helps in cracking WPA PSK and WEP.

2. Nmap

Nmap, also known as Network Mapper, it is an open source and free form of utility for the purpose of network discovery along with auditing of security. Nmap uses up the raw packets of IP for determining which hosts are available on the desired network, what are the services are being offered by those hosts, what are the operating systems that they are using, which type of firewall or packet filters are being used and various other characteristics. Many of the administrators of network and systems also use it for:

- Inventory of network
- Managing the schedules of service upgrade
- Monitoring the service or host uptime

3. THC Hydra

When you are required to crack one remote authentication service, THC Hydra can be used. It is capable of performing super-fast dictionary attacks in opposition to 50 or more protocols which includes HTTP, FTP, SMB and HTTPS. It can be used easily for the purpose of cracking into wireless networks, web scanners, packet crafters and many more.

4. Nessus

It is a form of remote scanning tool which is used for checking the security vulnerabilities of computers. It is not capable of blocking any form of vulnerabilities that the system of a computer has but it can easily sniff all of them out by running more than 1200 checks for vulnerability and also sends out alerts when it is required to make the security patches.

5. Wire Shark

It is an open-source analyzer of packet which anyone can use and that too free of charge. With the help of this tool, the user can easily see the network activities provided along with customizable reports, alerts, triggers and many more.

The Features of Kali Linux

Kali Linux is a form of Linux distribution that comes along with a wide range of tools which are pre-installed in the distribution. It has been designed for the targeted users for ease of functioning. Kali Linux is more or less like the other distributions of Linux but it comes along with some added features too that help in differentiating it from the others. Let's check out some of the most unique features of Kali Linux.

1. Live system

Unlike the other distributions of Linux, the primary ISO image that you are going to download will not only help in installing the OS but it can also be used just like a bootable form of live system. In simple words, Kali Linux can be used without even installing it in the system by just using the ISO image by booting the same. The live system of the distribution contains all the tools which are required by the penetration testers. So, in case your present system is not running on Kali Linux OS, you can easily use it by inserting the USB device and then reboot the same for running Kali Linux on your system.

2. Forensics mode

While performing any kind of forensic related work on the system, generally the users want to avoid any form of activity which might result in data alteration on the system which is being analyzed. Unfortunately, most of the modern- day environments of desktop tend to interfere with this form of objective and tries to auto-mount any form of the disk which it detects. In order to avoid this form of behavior, Kali Linux comes with the forensics mode which can be enabled from the menu of reboot and it will result in disabling all such features. The live system of Kali Linux turns out to be so useful only for the purpose of forensics as it is readily possible to reboot any system of computer into the system of Kali Linux without even accessing or doing any kind of modification in the hard disks.

3. Customized Kernel of Linux

Kali Linux is well-known for providing customized version of the recent kernel of Linux which is based on the latest version of Debian Unstable. This helps in ensuring solid support for hardware, precisely for the wide collection of wireless devices. The kernel of Linux gets patched with the support for wireless injection as some of the assessment tools regarding wireless security tends to rely on this form of feature. As most of the hardware devices need updated files of firmware, Kali Linux comes with the feature of installing the files by default along with all the firmware updates which are available in the non-free section of Debian.

4. Trustable OS

The users of this security distribution wants to know that whether or not it can be trusted and as it has been developed plain sight, it allows anyone to easily inspect the codes of the source. Kali Linux has been developed by a very small team of developers who always follow the required practices of security. The developers also upload the source packages in signed format.

5. Customizable

Each and every penetration tester has their own way of working and might not agree with the default configuration of the OS. Kali Linux is fully customizable which allows the users to customize the same according to their need. There are also various forms of live-build techniques that can be found online that helps in modifying the OS, install several other supplementary forms of files, run the arbitrary commands, install any other required packages and many more. The users can also customize the way in which the distribution functions.

CHAPTER THIRTEEN

THE INSTALLATION OF KALI LINUX

If you are thinking about pursuing information security for your career, the primary thing that you require is to have an operating system which is focused only on system security. With the help of a proper operating system, you can easily perform various forms of tedious and time- consuming jobs very easily and efficiently. In the present situation, there are various OS available which are based on Linux. Out of the several distributions that can be found today, Kali Linux is regarded as the best choice for the purpose of information security and penetration testing. It is being widely used by the professional penetration testers and the ethical hackers for performing various activities related to their field along with the assessment of network security.

Kali Linux is regarded as the leading distribution from the house of Linux which is also being used for auditing of security. Kali Linux is the only OS related to ethical hacking and network security that comes pre-packaged with several different types of tools related to the hacking of command line which is required for various tasks related to information security. The tasks in which Kali Linux is most commonly used are application security, penetration testing, forensics related to computer system and security of network. In simple terms, Kali Linux is the one and only and the ultimate operating system which has been designed for the ethical hackers.

People who are connected with the world of ethical hacking and penetration testing use Kali Linux for some specific reasons. Kali Linux comes with more than 600 tools for penetration testing. The best part is Kali Linux is 100% customizable. So, in case you are not liking the present configuration of Kali Linux, you can easily customize it in the way you want. Another interesting thing about Kali Linux is that it comes with multilingual support. Although the tools are written in English, this allows people from all provinces to use this OS using their own native language. It comes with the support of a wide collection of wireless devices. Kali Linux is such an OS which is developed in a secure form of environment. What makes Kali Linux so popular is the feature of being an open source nature of software which is free as well. It also comes with custom kernel which can also be patched for the purpose of injections.

How can you install Kali Linux?

The process of installing Kali Linux in your system is quite easy and simple. The users can also enjoy several options for installing the software. The most preferable options for installation are:

- Installation of Kali Linux by using hard disk
- Installation of Kali Linux by creating bootable Kali Linux USB Drive

- Installing Kali Linux by using software for virtualization like VirtualBox and VMware Installing Kali Linux by the process of dual booting along with the operating system

The most widely used options for installing Kali Linux are by using USB drive and installation by using VirtualBox or VMware. You need minimum 20 GB of free space in the hard disk of your system along with at least 4 GB of RAM if you are using VirtualBox or VMware. You will also require USB along with CD/DVD support.

Installing Kali Linux with the help of VMware

Before you want to run Kali Linux in your system, you will require a virtualization software at the very first place. There are various options available today when it comes to choosing a virtualization software. You can start by installing VMware or VirtualBox from the house of Oracle. After you have installed the virtualization software, you need to launch the same from the folder of applications.

Now you are required to download the installation file for Kali Linux which you can easily find from the download page in the official website of Kali Linux. You can choose the one which you think will be meeting your needs. Along with the download file in the download page, you will also come across a wide variety of hexadecimal numbers which are used for the security-related jobs. You are required to check the image integrity which you are going to download. You need to check fingerprint SHA- 256 for the file and then compare the same which has been provided on the download page of Kali Linux.

After you have downloaded the installation file for Kali Linux, you are required to launch the virtual machine now. For this, you need to open the homepage of VMware Workstation Pro and then select create a new virtual machine. After you have created a new virtual machine, you need to select the iso file of Kali Linux followed by the selection of the guest OS. You will also need to configure all the details of the virtual machine which is Kali Linux in this case. Now you can start the Kali Linux virtual machine simply by selecting the VM for Kali Linux and then selecting the power on button which is green in color.

After the virtual machine has powered up, a pop-up menu will be prompted in which you need to select the preferable mode of installation in the GRUB menu. You need to select the option graphical install. Click on continue. The next few screens will be asking you to choose your locale information like the preferred language in which you want Kali Linux to install, the location of your country along with the layout of your keyboard.

Once you are done with all the required locale information, the installer will automatically start to install some required additional components for the software and then will also configure the settings related to network. After the components have been installed, the installer will ask you to enter the hostname along with the domain name for the purpose of installation. You are required to provide each and every appropriate information for proper installation of the software and for continuing with the installation.

After you are done with all the above-mentioned steps, you will need to set up a password for your machine of Kali Linux and then hit the continue button. Make sure that you do not forget to set a password for your Kali Linux machine.

As you set up the password for your Kali Linux machine, the installer will then prompt you for setting up the time zone and will then pause the setup at the time of defining the disk partitions. The installer of the machine will give you four different choices regarding the disk partitions for the machine disk. In case you are not sure about partitioning your disk, the easiest option which is available for you is to select the option of Guided – Use Entire Disk which will be using up the entire disk space and will omit the process of disk partitioning. If you are an experienced user, you can select the option of manual partitioning for more granular options for configuration.

You will now require to select the partitioning disk. However, the most recommended option is to select the option for all files in one partition for all the new users. After you gave selected the partitioning disk, select continue. Now you will need to confirm all the changes that you have made to the disk on the machine of the host. Make sure that you do not continue with the process as it will be erasing all the data which is available on the disk. Once you confirm all the changes in the partition, the Kali Linux installer will start running the process of file installation. It might take a while and do not interrupt the process as the system will install everything automatically.

Once all the required files have been installed, the system will be asking you in case you want to set up any network for the purpose of obtaining the future updates and pieces of software. Make sure that you enable this function if you are going to use the repositories of Kali Linux in the future. The system will then configure the manager of package related files.

After this step, the system will be asking you to install the boot loader of GRUB. Click on yes and then select the device for writing up the required information of boot loader to the hard disk which is needed for booting Kali Linux. Once the installer has finished installing the boot loader of GRUB into the disk, select continue for finishing up the process of installation. It will then install some of the files at the final stage.

After you are done with all these steps, Kali Linux will be installed in your system and you can start using the same for the purpose of penetration testing and network security. You can also use Kali Linux in your system by simply creating a USB bootable drive without even installing the software in the system.

CHAPTER FOURTEEN

THE APPLICTAIONS AND USES OF KALI LINUX

Kali Linux is a well-known OS in the world of ethical hacking. While it is known that the prime focus of Kali Linux is on the summarized use for penetration testing along with security auditing, Kali Linux can also perform several other tasks apart from these two. Kali Linux has been designed in the form of a framework as it comes with various forms of tools which can cover various types of use cases. Some of the tools of Kali Linux can also be used in combination at the time of performing penetration testing.

For instance, it is possible to use Kali Linux on various types of computers such as on the system of the penetration tester, on the servers of the administrators of the system who wants to monitor their own network, on the systems or workstations of the analysts related to system forensics and also on the embedded form of devices generally along with the ARM CPUs which can be easily dropped in the range of the wireless network or which can also be plugged in the system of the targeted user. Many of the devices related to ARM also perform as great machines for the purpose of attacking which is mainly because of their small factors of formation along with the requirement very low power.

You can also deploy Kali Linux directly in the cloud for the purpose of quickly building a large farm of machines which are able to crack passwords and on the mobile phones along with tablets for allowing an efficient form of portable testing of penetration. But it does not end here; the penetration testers also require servers. The servers are required for using a software of collaboration within a large group of penetration testers, for setting up the web server to be used for campaigns related to phishing, for the purpose of running the tools related to vulnerability scanning and for various other interconnected jobs.

Once you are done with booting of Kali Linux, you will find out that the main menu of Kali Linux has been organized in accordance to various themes across the different forms of activities and tasks which are relevant to the penetration testers and other professionals of information security.

Tasks that can be performed with Kali Linux

Kali Linux helps in performing a wide range of tasks. Let's have a look at some of them.

1. Gathering of information

Kali Linux can be used for collecting various forms of data related to the targeted networks along with the structure of the same. It also helps in identifying the systems of computers, the operating systems of such computers along with all the services that the computer system runs. Kali Linux can be used for identifying the various potential sensitive parts within the system of information along with the extraction of all forms of listings from the services of a running directory.

2. Analysis of vulnerability

You can use Kali Linux for the purpose of quick testing of whether a remote or any local system has been affected by any known vulnerabilities or any form of configuration which is not at all secure in nature. The scanners of vulnerability use the databases which contain several signatures for the purpose of identifying the potential threats and vulnerabilities.

3. Analysis of web application

It helps in the identification of any form of misconfiguration along with weaknesses in the security system of the web applications. It is a very crucial task to identify and then mitigate such issues given that public availability of such applications makes the same the ideal form of targets for all the attackers.

4. Assessment of database

Database attacks are the most common form of vector for the attackers that include attacks such as SQL injection to attacks in the credentials. Kali Linux provides various tools which can be used for testing the vector of attacks which ranges from data extraction to SQL injection along with analysis of the same.

5. Password attacks

The systems connected with authentication are always vulnerable to the attacks of the attackers. A wide array of tools can be found in Kali Linux which ranges from online tools of password attack to the offline tools against the systems of hashing or encryption.

6. Wireless form of attacks

Wireless networks are pervasive in nature. This means that they are always a common vector of attack for the attackers. Kali Linux comes with a wide range of support related to various cards of the network which makes Kali Linux an obvious choice for the attacks in opposition to the several wireless network types.

7. Reverse engineering

Reverse engineering is a very important form of activity which is being used for various purposes. In providing support for the various forms of offensive activities, reverse engineering is one of the prime methods which is being used for identification of the vulnerabilities and also for tracking the development of exploitation. On the side of defense, it is also being used for analyzing the malware which is employed for the targeted attacks. Within this capacity, the aim is to identify the prime capabilities of a given set of tradecrafts.

8. Tools for exploitation

Exploitation is the act of taking advantage of any form of existing vulnerability in a system which allows the attacker to gain complete control of a remote form of device or machine. This form of access can also be used by the attackers for further privileges of escalation of attacks which are done either on any form of machine which is accessible to the local network or on the machine which has been compromised. This category of Kali Linux function comes with various tools along with utilities which help in simplifying the overall process writing up your very own form of exploits.

9. Spoofing and sniffing

Gaining overall access to that packet of data which is travelling across any network is always advantageous for the attackers. Kali Linux can provide you with various tools for the purpose of spoofing which will allow you to imitate any legitimate user along with the sniffing tools which will allow you to analyze and also capture the available pool of data directly from the network wire. When spoofing as well as sniffing tools are used together, it can turn out to be very powerful.

10. Post exploitation

Once you have been successful in gaining all-over access to the target system, you might want to maintain the same level of accessibility to the system along with extended control simply by moving laterally over the network. You can find various tools in Kali Linux for assisting you in your goals regarding post exploitation.

11. Forensics

The live boot environments of Forensic Linux have been very famous in the recent years. Kali Linux comes with a large number of very popular tools of forensics which are based on Linux which will allow you to perform everything, starting from the initial stage of triage to imaging of data along with full analysis of the system and lastly management of case.

12. Tools of reporting

A test of penetration can only be declared as successful once all the findings of the test have been properly reported. This category of tools from Kali Linux helps in composing the collected data which has been gathered by the use of tools for information gathering, finding out various non-obvious form of relationships and also bringing together everything in several reports.

13. Tools for social engineering

When the technical aspect of a system is secured properly, there are chances of exploiting the behavior of human beings as a vector of attack. When provided with the perfect influence, human beings can be induced frequently for taking various actions which ultimately leads to the compromising of the security of a system environment. Did the USB drive which was just now plugged in by the secretary contain any form of harmful PDF? Or did the UDB drive just installed a form of Trojan horse backdoor? Was the website of banking which was used by the accountant just now was a normal expected form of website or a copy of a website for the purpose of phishing attack? Kali Linux comes with various tools that can help you in aiding all these forms of attacks.

- **Services for system:** Kali Linux can provide with tools which will allow you to initiate and also stop various applications which run in the background as the services for the system

Coordinating tasks of Kali Linux

Kali Linux helps in coordinating several tasks and also helps in balancing the coordination between the software and hardware of a system. The first and foremost task of Kali Linux is to control the hardware components of the computer system. It helps in detecting along with figuring out the various hardware components when the computer turns on or also when any new device is installed. It helps in making the hardware components available for the various higher level of software with the help of a simplified form of program interface so that the applications can take all-round advantage of the connected devices without the need of addressing any detail like in which extension slot is the option board plugged in. The interface of programming also comes with a layer of abstraction which allows various software to work seamlessly with the hardware.

What makes Kali Linux different from others?

Kali Linux has been specifically designed for gearing up the functioning of the penetration testers and also for the purpose of security auditing. For achieving this, various core changes have also been implemented for Kali Linux which reflects all of these requirements:

1. Root access by design, single-user

Because of the normal nature of the audits regarding system auditing, Kali Linux has been designed in such a way which can be used in the scenario of single root access. Most of the tools which are employed for the purpose of penetration testing needs escalated form of privileges and as it is typically sound policy for enabling the root privileges when required, during the use cases to which Kali Linux is aimed to, this whole approach might turn out to be a huge burden.

2. The services of network disabled by default

Kali Linux comes with systematic hooks which disables the services of a network by default. Such hooks allow the users to install several Kali Linux services while also making sure that the distributions also remains completely safe and secure by default no matter which type of packages has been installed. Other additional services like Bluetooth are also kept in the blacklist by default settings.

3. Custom kernel of Linux

Kali Linux uses up upstream form of the kernel which is patched for the purpose of wireless injection.

4. A set of trusted and minimal repositories

The absolute key of Kali Linux is to maintain the integrity of a given system, given all the goals and aims of Kali Linux. With the prime aim in mind, the complete collection of sources of upstream software which are used by Kali Linux is kept as minimum as possible. Many of the new users of Kali Linux gets tempted to add the extra repositories to the sources. List. But, by doing so, it leads to the risk of breaking the installation of Kali Linux.

It is not correct to suggest that everyone should be using Kali Linux. Kali Linux is been designed particularly for the security specialists. It comes with a unique nature because of which Kali Linux is not a recommended distribution for those who are not at all familiar with the functioning of Linux or are looking out for some general form of Linux distribution for their desktop, for gaming, designing of website and many more. Even for the experienced users of Linux, Kali Linux might come along with certain challenges which are generally set up due to preserving the security of the systems.

CHAPTER FIFTEEN

USING KALI LINUX FOR HACKING

As we all know by now that Kali Linux has been designed especially for the purpose of penetration testing and security auditing, it can also be used for the purpose of ethical hacking which is required while performing penetration testing and other security checks. Kali Linux comes packed with a huge number of tools which helps in the venture of security infrastructure testing and other forms of testing for securing an organization or company.

Who all uses Kali Linux and why?

Kali Linux can be regarded as the most unique form of OS which can be found today as serves as a platform which can be used up by both the good guys and the bad guys. The administrators of security along with the black hat hackers all use this platform for meeting their needs. One uses this system for the purpose of preventing and detecting breaches in security infrastructure while the other uses this OS for identifying and thereby exploiting the security breaches. The huge number of tools which comes packed with Kali Linux can be regarded as the Swiss Knife for the toolbox of the security professionals. The professionals who widely use Kali Linux are:

1. Security Administrators

The administrators of security come with the responsibility of safeguarding the information and data of the concerned institution. The security administrators widely use Kali Linux for the purpose of ensuring that there are no forms of vulnerabilities in the environment of the security infrastructure.

2. Network administrators

The network administrators come with the responsibility of maintaining a secure and efficient network. Kali Linux is used by the network administrators for the purpose of auditing of network. For instance, Kali Linux can easily detect the access points of rogue.

3. Architects of network

Such people are responsible for the designing of a secure environment for a network. They use Kali Linux for auditing the internal network designs and makes sure that nothing has been misconfigured or overlooked.

4. Penetration testers

The penetration testers use Kali Linux for auditing the security environments and also perform reconnaissance for the corporate environments which they are bound to take care of.

5. CISO

The Chief Information Security Officer takes help of Kali Linux for the purpose of internal auditing of the environment of their infrastructure and finds out if any new form of application or configurations of rogue has been installed in the environment.

6. Forensic engineers

Kali Linux comes along with a mode of forensics which allows the forensic engineers for performing discovery of data along with data recovery in various instances.

7. White hat hackers

The white hat hackers or the ethical hackers are similar to the penetration testers who use Kali Linux for auditing and for finding out vulnerabilities which might be present within a security environment.

8. Black hat hackers

The black hat hackers use Kali Linux for finding out vulnerabilities in a system and then exploiting the same. Kali Linux comes with various applications of social engineering which can be easily used by the black hat hackers for compromising an individual or an organization.

9. Grey hat hackers

The grey hat hackers also use Kali Linux just like the black hat as well as the white hat hackers.

10. Computer enthusiasts

It is a very generic form of term but any person who is interested in getting to know more about computers and networking can use the system of Kali Linux for the purpose of learning more about networking, information technology and common form of vulnerabilities.

Process of hacking

Kali Linux is very popular as a hacking platform. The word "hacking" might not always be negative as it is also being used for various other jobs other than exploitation. By gathering immense knowledge about the process of hacking with Kali Linux, you can learn how to perform for vulnerability check and how to fix them as well in case you want to choose ethical hacking as your career option. The process of hacking with Kali Linux is similar to that of a general hacking process in which a hacker tries to get into the server of an organization or company and thereby gain all forms of access to the data which is stored in the servers. The process of hacking can be divided into five different steps.

1. Reconnaissance

This is regarded as the very first step while starting with the process of hacking. In this step, the hacker tends to use all the available means for the purpose of collection of all forms of information about the targeted system. It includes various phases such as target identification, determining the target IP address range, available network, records of DNS and many others. In simple terms, the hacker gathers all contacts of a website or server. This can be achieved by the hacker by using various forms of search engines like maltego, researching about the system of the target, for instance, a server or website or by utilizing various other forms of tools like HTTP Track for the purpose of downloading a complete website for enumeration at later stages. After the hacker is done with all these steps, he can figure out the employee names, the positions of the employees along with the designated email addresses of the employees.

2. Scanning

After the collection of all forms of information regarding the target, the hacker starts with the second phase which is scanning. The hackers utilize several forms of tools in this phase such as dialers, port scanner, network mappers, scanners of vulnerability and many others. As Kali Linux comes pre-loaded with a huge bunch of tools, the hackers won't even face any form of difficulty during this phase. The hackers try to find out that information about the target system which can actually help in moving ahead with an attack such as IP addresses, the accounts of the users and computer names. As the hackers get done with basic information collection, they start looking out for the other possible avenues of attack within the target system. The hackers can select various tools from Kali Linux for the purpose of network mapping such as Nmap. The hackers try to find out automated email reply system or simply by basing on the information which has been gathered by them. The hackers move to the next step which includes emailing the staffs of the company regarding various queries, such as mailing the HR of a company about a detailed enquiry on job vacancy.

3. Gaining overall access

This phase is regarded as the most important of all when it comes to hacking. In this phase, the attacker attempts to create the design of the network blueprint which has been targeted. It is created with all the relevant information which has been collected by the hacker. After the hackers finish the phase of enumeration and scanning, the step that comes now is gaining access of the targeted network which is based completely on the information collected. It might happen that the hacker wants to use phishing attack. He might try to take it safe and thus use only a very simple attack of phishing for the purpose of gaining access. The hacker can decide to get into the targeted system from the IT department of the organization.

The attacker might also get to know that some recent hiring has been done by the company and it can help in speeding up the procedure. For the phishing attack, the hacker might send out emails of phishing by using the actual address of email of the CTO of the company with the use of a unique form of program and will send out the mails to all the technicians. The email which will be used for the purpose of phishing will be containing a website which will help in gathering all the required user ids and passwords for the purpose of logging in. The hacker can also use other choices like phone app, website mail or some other platform for the purpose of sending out mail of phishing to the users and then asking the individuals for logging in to a new Google portal with the use of their provided credentials.

When the hackers decide to use such a technique, they have a special type of program which runs in the background in their system which is called Social Engineering

Toolkit. It is used by attackers for sending out the emails with the address of the server to the users directly after masking the server address with the help of bitly or tinyurl. The attackers can also use other methods for gaining access to the system such as by making a reverse TCP/IP shell in the PFD format file which can be created by the use of Metasploit. The attackers can also employ overflows of buffer for the attacks which are based on stacking or hijacking of the sessions which ultimately results in gaining overall access to the targeted server.

4. Maintaining the access to the server

After the hacker has gained access to the target server, he will try to keep the access to the server as it is and keeping it safe for future exploitation and attacks. When a hacker gets access to an overall system, he can use the hijacked system as his own personal base and use the same for launching several other attacks to the other systems. After a hacker gains access to a targeted system and ultimately owns the same, the hijacked system is called a zombie system. The hacker gains access to a whole new array of email addresses and accounts and can start using those for testing other form attacks right from the same domain. For the purpose hiding in the system, the hacker also tries to create a brand-new administrator account and tries to get dissolved in the system.

For safety purposes, the hacker also starts to find out and identify those accounts in a system which has not been used by the organization for a long period of time. After the hacker finds out such form of accounts, he changes all the login passwords of the old accounts and elevates all form of privileges right to the administrator of the system like a secondary account for the purpose of having safe access to the network which has been targeted. The hacker can also begin to send out various emails to the other users within an organization which might contain exploited form of files in the PDF format with the reverse shell scheme for extending his all- round access within the system. After all these, the hacker waits for some time to make sure that no form of disturbance has been detected in the system and after getting sure of the same, he starts to create copies of the available pool of user data like contacts, files, messages, emails and various other forms of data for using them in the later stage.

5. Clearance of track

Before starting a system attack, the hackers plan out their whole pathway for the attack along with their planning for identity so that if any discrepancy occurs no one can trace them up. The hackers start doing so by altering their MAC address and then run the same system across a VPN so that their identity can be covered up easily. After the hackers have achieved their target, they begin with clearance of their pathways and tracks. This complete phase includes various things such as clearing of the temp files, mails which has been sent, the logs of the servers and various other things. The hacker also tries to make sure that there is no form of alert message from the email provider which can alarm the targeted organization regarding any form of unauthorized or unrecognized login in the system.

A penetration tester follows all these steps for the purpose of testing the vulnerabilities of a system and making sure that those which are available in the system are mended properly.

CHAPTER SIXTEEN

PORT SCANNING USING KALI LINUX

Identification of the open ports on the targeted system is essential for defining the surface of attack of the target. The open ports of the target correspond with the networked services which are running on the system. Errors in programming or flaws in implementation can result in making all these services very much susceptible to the attacks and can also lead to compromise of the overall system. For the purpose of determining the most probable vectors of attack, you are required to enumerate all the ports which are in open condition on all the systems of remote form within the scope of the project. The open number of ports also corresponds with the services which can be easily addressed with the help of either TCP or UDP traffic.

Both UDP and TCP are protocols of transport. TCP or Transmission Control Protocol is the one which is more commonly used than UDP and also provides communication which is connection- oriented. UDP or User Datagram Protocol is a protocol which non-connection oriented in nature which is also sometimes used along with the services in which transmission speed is more important than the integrity of data. The form of penetration testing which used for the purpose of enumerating such services is known as port scanning. Such technique helps in yielding enough amount of information for the purpose of identifying whether the service is being associated with any port on the server or on the device.

UDP Port Scanning

As TCP is more frequently used than UDP as a protocol 0f transport layer, services which are operated by UDP are most often forgotten. In spite of the normal tendency of overlooking the services of UDP, it is also critical for these services to be enumerated for acquiring an overall understanding of the surface of attack of any form of target. The form of scanning with UDP might often turn out to be tedious, challenging and time-consuming as well. For gaining overall insight into the functioning of these tools it is very essential to understand the two exactly different approaches of UDP scanning which is used.

The first technique which is used is to rely on the ICMP port unreachable responses exclusively. This form of scanning relies on those assumptions which the UDP ports which are not linked with the live service will return ICMP port unreachable response. Lack of this response is taken as the indication of a live form of service. Although this form of approach might turn out to be very effective in various circumstances, there are also chances of the same of returning inaccurate form of results in the cases in which the host is unable to generate port unreachable response or the replies of port unreachable is either filtered by any form of firewall or are rate limited. It also comes with an alternative in which service specific probes are used for attempting soliciting of a response which will indicate that the service which was expected is running on the port which is targeted. Although this form of approach might turn out to be very effective, it is also very time-consuming at the same time.

TCP Port Scanning

TCP port scanning includes various approaches such as connect scanning, stealth scanning along with zombie scanning. For understanding how all these techniques of scanning work, you need to understand how the connections of TCP are established and also maintained. TCP is a form of protocol which is connection-oriented. Data is transported over TCP only after a successful connection has been created in between the two systems. The process which is associated with the creation of connection of TCP is often called three-way handshake. This term alludes from the three different steps which are involved in the process of connection.

A packet of TCP SYN is sent from that device which wants to establish connection along with the device port which it wants to connect with. If the associate service with the port which the device wants to connect to accepts the connection, the port will be replying to the system which is requesting the connection with a packet of TCP that comes with both ACK and SYN bits activated. The connection is successful when the requesting system responds back to the port with a response of TCP ACK. These three steps in total sums up the three-step process which is required for the establishment of a session of TCP between two systems. All the techniques of TCP port scanning will be performing some sort of variation of this entire process for the purpose of identifying the live services on the remote form of hosts.

Both the process of stealth scanning and connect scanning are quite easy to understand. The process of connect scanning is used up for establishing a complete TCP connection every port which is being scanned. This is done for each of the ports which are scanned for completing the three-way handshake. When a connection is established successfully, the port is determined to be

in the open state. However, in the case of stealth scanning, a full connection is not established. Stealth scanning is often referred to as SYN scanning or also half open scanning.

For each and every port which are scanned, one single packet of SYN is sent out to the port of destination and all the ports which replies with a packet of SYN+ACK are taken as to be running the live form of services. As no final form of ACK is sent out from the system which initiated the connection, the connection is left out as half open. This is known as stealth scanning as the solutions of logging which only records the connections which are established do not record any form of evidence of the performed scan.

The final method which comes with TCP scanning is the zombie scanning. The prime goal of zombie scanning is to map all the open form of ports on a system of remote nature without even producing any form of evidence which you have had an interaction with the system. The principles on which the functioning of zombie scanning depends are complex in nature. You can carry out zombie scanning by following these steps.

Start by identifying the remote system for the zombie. The system which you are going to identify needs to have these characteristics:

- It is in idle form and it doesn't actively communicate with the other systems which are available on the network.

- It needs to use an incremental form of IPID sequence.

- Then you will need to send in a packet of SYN+ACK to the zombie and then record the initial value of IPID.

- Send in a packet of SYN along with a source of the spoofed IP address of the system of zombie to the target system of scan.

- Depending on the port status on the target scan, any of the following will happen:

In case the port is in open state, the scan target will be returning a packet of SYN+ACK to the host of zombie which it thinks sent out the original request of SYN. In such a case, the host of zombie will be responding to the unsolicited form of SYN+ACK packet with a packet of RST and then increment the value of IPID by one. In case the port is in the closed state, the scan target will be returning a response of RST to the host of zombie which it thinks sent out the original request of SYN. The packet of RST will be soliciting no form of response from the host of zombie and the value of IPID will therefore not be increased.

Send in another packet of SYN+ACK to the host of zombie and then evaluate the final value of IPID of the RST response which has been returned. In case the value has been increased by one, the port on the target scan is closed and in case the value has been increased by two the port on the target scan is in open state.

For performing a zombie form of scan, an initial request of SYN/ACK is required to be sent to the system of zombie for the purpose of determining the current value of IPID within the returned packet of RST. A spoofed packet of SYN is then sent out to the scan target along with a form of source IP address of the system of zombie. As the zombie actually did not send out the initial request of SYN, it will be interpreting the response of SYN/ACK as being unsolicited and then send a packet of RST back to the system of target and thus increasing the value of IPID by one. At the final stage, another packet of SYN/ACK needs to be sent to the system of zombie which will return a packet of RST and then increase the value of IPID by one.

CHAPTER SEVENTEEN

PENETRATION TESTING

Each and every infrastructure of IT comes with some weak points which can ultimately lead to some serious attack and can be used for the purpose of stealing and manipulating data. Only one thing can be done in such situations which can help in preventing the hackers from entering the system. You need to perform regular checks of the infrastructure of your security and make sure that there is no form of vulnerabilities present in the structure. Penetration testing helps in finding out the vulnerabilities along with the several weak points in a system. As the owner or administrator of a network, they can always have some advantage over the hackers as they are bound to know the topology of network, the components of infrastructure, the services, the probable points of attack, the executed services and many more. Penetration testing is done within a real and secure environment so that in case any vulnerability is found, you can mend the same and secure the system.

Penetration testing in details

As the name goes by, penetration testing is the process of testing a system to find out whether penetration by any third party is possible in the system or not.

Penetration testing is often mixed up with ethical hacking as both are somewhat similar in features and functioning. The motive of are also the same but a very thin line differentiates the two. In penetration testing, the tester scans

for any form of vulnerability in the system, malicious form of content, risks and flaws in the concerned system. Penetration testing can be performed either in an online network or server or a computer system as well. Penetration testing comes with the goal of strengthening the security system of an organization for the motive of properly defending the security of a system. Unlike hacking, penetration testing legal in nature and is done with all forms of official workings. If used in the proper way it can do wonders. Penetration testing can be considered as a significant part of ethical hacking.

Penetration testing needs to be performed at regular intervals as it comes with the power of improving the capabilities of a system and also improves the strategies related to cyber security. Various types of malicious content are created for the purpose of fishing out the weak points which are available within a program, application or system. For effective testing, the malicious content which is created is spread across the entire network for vulnerability testing. The process of penetration testing might not be able to handle all the concerns related to security; however, it can help in minimizing the probable chances of any form of attack. It helps in making sure that a company is safe from all forms of vulnerabilities and thus protecting the same from cyber-attacks. It also helps in checking whether or not the defensive measures are enough for the organization and which of the security measures are required to be changed for the motive of decreasing the vulnerability of the system.

Penetration testing is really helpful in pointing out the strengths along with the weaknesses in the structure of an organization at any one given point of time. You need to note that this whole process if not at all casual in nature. It includes rigorous planning, granting of the required permissions from the concerned management and then initiating the process.

Security scanners

The process of penetration testing starts after an overview of the complete organization has been collected and then the process of searching for the specific weak points starts. For performing all these, you are required to use a security scanner. Depending on the type and nature of the security scanners, the tools can actually help in checking an entire system or network for the weak points which are known. One of the most comprehensive forms of tool for security scanning is OpenVAS. This tool comes with the idea of a huge number of vulnerabilities and can also check for the defenses. After the OpenVAS tool has identified all the open form of tools, you can easily use Nmap for discovering the details. A tool like Wireshark will allow you to find out any form of content which is critical in nature along with any critical form of network activity which can point out certain patterns of attack.

The classic form of Wireshark tool is also useful in identifying the bottlenecks which can indicate the attacks of the hackers and also requires a continuous check. In the world of corporate organizations, the applications which are based on the web often depend on MySQL, Apache and

stack of PHP. All these platforms dominate the entire landscape. Such platforms are the favorite targets of the hackers as they usually come with great opportunities of attacks. Kali Linux comes with around two dozen tools which specialize in web application testing. Such scanners can be easily found in the menu of Web Application Analysis. The w3af and Burp Suite are regarded as the best tools of the lot.

Burp Suite helps in the identification and testing of the vulnerabilities and is quite easy to use. Brute force attack can be launched from the module of the intruder which takes help of the request records which are grouped in the proxy intercept tab for the purpose of injecting the required payload in the system of the web. It also helps in detecting configurations of poor security. Configuration of incorrect nature of the security settings can take place at any of the levels of the stack of application. For the purpose of detecting these vulnerabilities, Burp Suite starts with the identification of the target and then executes the Spider command from the menu of context. The outputs which can be found from the scans can help you in finding out the misconfigurations in the system.

Generally, a great amount of caution is needed at the time of product system analyzing with the security scanners which are not designed in a way for getting handled by the kid hands. Although various actions serve for identifying the points of attack, you can expect that the concerned system which is being tested might also get affected. So, you are required to perform all these tests within mirrored form of systems. Generally, the mirrors of the systems are secured by the firewall and IDSs of the system of production, so you can also check the overall effectiveness of the protection mechanisms which are existing already. Several forms of tools can run in various modes which might make it difficult for the IDSs to properly detect the scans. While running in the intelligent modes, they often fail to get detected.

Sounding the weak points

After you have found out where are the gaps in the, the next step that you need to perform is to sound all of them out. An important portion of the penetration tests is the use of the tools which helps in stimulating as many patterns of attack as possible. Metasploit can be regarded as the most widely used form of tool for penetration testing and is also a great tool for the penetration testers.

FINAL NOTES FROM THE AUTHOR

Thank you for taking the time to read *Programming for Beginners 2025*. I hope this book has provided you with the foundational knowledge and confidence to embark on your programming journey. Learning to code is a skill that opens doors to creativity, innovation, and problem-solving.

As you continue to explore the world of programming, remember that growth comes with consistent practice and curiosity. The learning process can be challenging, but each challenge you overcome brings you closer to mastering the art of coding.

Whether you plan to build your own projects, advance your career, or simply enjoy the satisfaction of creating something from scratch, I encourage you to keep pushing forward. Don't be afraid to experiment, make mistakes, and learn from them. The programming community is vast and welcoming—there are countless resources, communities, and mentors eager to support your growth.

I would love to hear about your progress, feedback, and any projects you build as a result of reading this book. Feel free to reach out and share your experiences.

Happy coding, and may your journey be filled with creativity and discovery.

Warm regards,

Grant D. Harper

CONCLUSION

As we come to the end of *Programming for Beginners 2025*, it's essential to reflect on the journey you have just undertaken. From learning the very basics of programming to diving into real-world applications, you have built a solid foundation that will serve as a launching pad for your continued growth and mastery in the field.

Throughout this book, you have explored core programming concepts such as variables, data types, loops, conditionals, and functions. You have delved into the essentials of data analysis, learned how to manipulate data using powerful libraries like NumPy and Pandas, and visualized data effectively with Matplotlib and Plotly. Moreover, you've been introduced to the principles of machine learning with Scikit-Learn and practiced applying these concepts through practical examples and exercises.

The progression from learning syntax and theory to building actual projects is a crucial step in becoming proficient in programming. As you applied your knowledge to real-world scenarios, you developed not only technical skills but also the critical thinking and problem-solving abilities that are essential for success in this field.

The Road Ahead

This book is just the beginning. Programming is a vast and ever-evolving discipline. The skills you have acquired here are fundamental, but there is always more to learn. As you continue your journey, consider exploring advanced topics such as:

- **Web Development:** Build dynamic websites and applications using frameworks like Django or Flask for Python.

- **Data Science and Machine Learning:** Continue enhancing your skills in data analysis, model building, and deployment.

- **Artificial Intelligence (AI):** Dive deeper into neural networks, natural language processing, and AI-driven solutions.

- **Mobile App Development:** Learn how to create mobile applications for Android, iOS, or cross-platform tools like React Native.

- **Game Development:** Explore the creative world of building games using libraries like Pygame or engines like Unity.

No matter which path you choose, remember that persistence and practice are key. Programming is not about memorizing code; it's about understanding principles, developing logic, and finding creative solutions to problems. The more you code, the better you will become.

Continuous Learning

Technology changes rapidly, and programmers must adapt to stay relevant. Continuously learning new tools, languages, and frameworks is essential. The programming community is a rich resource—there are countless tutorials, forums, and experts ready to assist you. Whether through online courses, coding bootcamps, or peer mentorship, you will always have opportunities to expand your knowledge.

Embracing Challenges and Celebrating Success

As you move forward, you will undoubtedly encounter obstacles. Embrace them. Each bug you solve, each concept you master, and each project you complete is a testament to your growth and resilience. Celebrate your successes, no matter how small they may seem.

Final Thoughts

Programming is a skill that empowers you to transform ideas into reality. It is a tool that can be applied across industries, from web development and data science to AI and game development. Most importantly, it is a journey of creativity, persistence, and lifelong learning.

I encourage you to keep coding, keep learning, and keep pushing yourself beyond your comfort zone. The possibilities are endless, and the future belongs to those who dare to create.

I will appreciate if you can give this book a positive review to help new readers know how helpful this book will be.

Thank you for allowing me to guide you through this journey. I hope this book has inspired and equipped you to continue building your skills and creating something meaningful.

Best wishes for your future programming endeavors!

Warm regards,

Grant D. Harper

Printed in Dunstable, United Kingdom